I0517804

wisdom

MAKING GODLY DECISIONS

SKINNY BROWN DOG
MEDIA
EST. 2013
ATLANTA | PUNTA DEL ESTE

Published by Skinny Brown Dog Media
Atlanta, GA /Punta del Este, Uruguay

For Information, Contact:
Distributed by Skinny Brown Dog Media
SkinnyBrownDogMedia.com
Email: Info@SkinnyBrownDogMedia.com

Wisdom: Making Godly Decisions
By Eric G Reid
Part of the Whole Life Devotional Series

Library of Congress Cataloging in Publication Data
ISBN (eBook)   978-1-965235-36-2
ISBN (trade paperback)   978-1-965235-33-1
ISBN (case laminate)   978-1-965235-35-5
ISBN (Hardback)   978-1-965235-34-8

DEDICATION

To Mum,
Queen of Kitchen Table Wisdom
For all the eye-rolls I gave you,
And all the lectures I'm now repeating.
Your words, once ignored, now guide me.

This book: part your wisdom,
part my stubborn learning,
part timeless biblical truth.

All my love and a belated "you were right"s,
Your slow-but-eventually-got-there kid

*"Listen, my son, to your father's instruction and
do not forsake your mother's teaching."*
—Proverbs 1:8 (NIV)

CONTENTS

Wisdom vii
Why This Study? ix
The Importance of Wisdom xi
What Can Be Gained? xii
How to Use This Devotional xv

WEEK 1:
Embracing Godly Wisdom for Life's Decisions

Day 1: Making Godly Decisions Through Discernment 5
Day 2: The Consequences of Wisdom Ignored 11
Day 3: The Wisdom of Humility .17
Day 4: The Power of Listening 21
Day 5: Seeking Counsel 26
Week 1 Reflection 31
Prayer. 34

WEEK 2:
Living Wisely in Everyday Life

Day 1: Wisdom in Relationships .41
Day 2: Wisdom in Stewardship. .46
Day 3: Wisdom in Work and Career 50
Day 4: Wisdom in Trials 54
Day 5: Wisdom in Speech 58
Week 2 Reflection 63
Prayer. 66

WEEK 3:
Wisdom and Faith

Day 1: Trusting God's Plan .73
Day 2: Walking in Faith and Wisdom 78
Day 3: Wisdom in Patience and Waiting 83
Day 4: Faith Over Fear 88
Day 5: Embracing Godly Wisdom 93
Week 3 Reflection 98
Prayer. 101

Preparing for the Future 103
Prayer for Wisdom: Making Godly Decisions. 115
Additional Resources for Wisdom: Making Godly Decisions 117
About the Author. 121
About the Whole Life Devotional Series 123
I AM 127

WISDOM

In life, we all face moments where we stand at a crossroads, wondering which path to take. Whether big or small, every decision shapes our lives and can have lasting effects. As believers, our goal is to make decisions that align with God's will, but this is not always easy in a world that constantly pulls us in different directions. That's why the pursuit of godly wisdom is essential. It's the anchor that helps us navigate the complexities of life with clarity, purpose, and peace.

Now more than ever, we are surrounded by an overwhelming amount of knowledge. With the rise of artificial intelligence, online information, and constant media input, it's easy to confuse the accumulation of knowledge with wisdom. We've become experts in obtaining facts, but facts alone don't equip us for wise living. Knowledge is knowing that a tomato is a fruit; wisdom is knowing not to put it in a fruit salad.

The difference between knowledge and wisdom is profound. Knowledge is the accumulation of information—data, facts, and figures. It's something that can be easily accessed in today's world with just a click or voice command. But wisdom, on the other hand, is the application of that knowledge in a way that honors God. Wisdom discerns not only what is right and wrong but when and how to act upon that knowledge in accordance with God's will.

The Bible speaks to this difference when it says, "For the Lord gives wisdom; from His mouth come knowledge and understanding"

(Proverbs 2:6). God doesn't just want us to know things; He wants us to apply those things in a way that glorifies Him and brings blessings into our lives. It's about discerning His voice amid the noise of the world and making choices that reflect His heart and His ways.

While knowledge can puff us up and make us feel self-reliant, wisdom humbles us, reminding us that God's understanding far exceeds our own. Proverbs 3:5-6 tells us, "*Trust in the Lord with all your heart and lean not on your own understanding; in all your ways submit to Him, and He will make your paths straight.*" Wisdom is not self-reliant but God-reliant.

The aim of this devotional is to help you tap into that wisdom and make choices that reflect God's heart in every area of your life. Wisdom is not just knowing the right thing but doing the right thing at the right time for the right reason. It's not about the volume of facts we possess, but the depth of insight we gain from the Holy Spirit.

As we embark on this journey together, remember this: wisdom is available to anyone who seeks it. James 1:5 promises, "*If any of you lacks wisdom, you should ask God, who gives generously to all without finding fault, and it will be given to you.*" Let's ask God for that wisdom as we step forward in faith, trusting that He will guide us to make godly decisions that will impact not only our lives but the lives of those around us.

WHY THIS STUDY?

The Bible makes no secret about the immense value of wisdom: *"If any of you lacks wisdom, you should ask God, who gives generously to all without finding fault, and it will be given to you"* (James 1:5). But let me ask you this—are we really seeking that wisdom? Not just nodding our heads in agreement when the sermon touches on it, but truly seeking it out and pursuing it in our daily lives? Here's the truth: wisdom isn't just a head full of knowledge. It's much more. It's about how we apply that knowledge in a way that honors God and aligns with His perfect will.

This study exists because, quite simply, we need wisdom. Godly wisdom is not just a "nice to have"; it's essential for navigating the complexities of our world. Every day, whether we realize it or not, we're making decisions that will affect not just ourselves, but our families, our communities, and even our churches. From the financial choices we make, to the dynamics of our relationships, to the direction of our careers, every decision is a step toward a future that can either honor God or drift away from Him.

Let's face it—life's decisions are more complicated than ever. We're living in a world that is constantly bombarding us with information, opinions, and pressures. But wisdom isn't found in following the loudest voice or taking the path of least resistance. No, true wisdom is grounded in God's Word, rooted in His truth, and applied in the everyday moments of our lives.

That's why this devotional is designed not just to teach you about wisdom, but to guide you into living it out—daily. We're not talking about abstract concepts or vague ideals. We're talking about real-life decisions. Decisions like how to manage your money, how to approach your relationships, how to grow in your spiritual life, and how to live out your calling with integrity.

Each step of this journey is aimed at helping you make those decisions with confidence, knowing that your choices are aligned with the timeless truths of Scripture and guided by the Holy Spirit. So, as we begin this study together, let's commit to asking God for wisdom every single day—because He promises to give it generously when we seek it with open hearts.

THE IMPORTANCE OF WISDOM

Wisdom is the ability to discern what is right and to act upon it. It's not simply knowing the difference between right and wrong, but also knowing when and how to apply God's principles in our everyday lives. The world teaches us to lean on our own understanding, to trust in our abilities or circumstances, but the Bible instructs us otherwise: "Trust in the Lord with all your heart and lean not on your own understanding; in all your ways submit to Him, and He will make your paths straight" (Proverbs 3:5-6).

When we rely on godly wisdom, we're not swayed by the trends and pressures of society. Instead, we're rooted in eternal truths that never change. Wisdom enables us to live lives of integrity, purpose, and joy, even when the world around us is uncertain. It strengthens our faith, deepens our trust in God, and ultimately draws us closer to His will for our lives.

In our fast-paced, decision-heavy world, it's easy to be overwhelmed by the sheer number of choices we must make. Without wisdom, we may end up relying on impulsive decisions, influenced more by emotion or circumstance than by God's Word. This study will remind you of the significance of stepping back, seeking God's guidance, and making decisions that honor Him.

WHAT CAN BE GAINED?

By engaging with this study, you're not just filling your mind with more knowledge—you're stepping into a deeper understanding of what it means to live wisely in a world overflowing with noise, distractions, and conflicting voices. You'll learn to:

- Discern between worldly knowledge and godly wisdom. In a culture that glorifies information overload, we'll explore how wisdom is something much deeper than mere facts—it's the divine application of truth in every situation.
- Apply biblical truths to real-life situations. Wisdom doesn't exist in a vacuum. It's about taking what God has taught us in His Word and using it to make decisions that honor Him in our daily lives—whether in our relationships, our work, or our personal struggles.
- Approach decision-making with confidence, knowing that God is guiding you. One of the beautiful things about godly wisdom is the peace it brings. As we grow in wisdom, we can make decisions with a sense of calm assurance that we're walking the path God has set for us.
- Develop spiritual disciplines that foster wisdom. Practices like prayer, meditating on God's Word, and seeking counsel from

wise, mature believers are essential. These aren't just spiritual "extras"—they are core habits that help wisdom take root in our lives.

But here's the thing: wisdom is never just for your benefit. True, godly wisdom always has an outward effect. It changes your relationships, shapes your influence, and empowers your ability to serve others. The wisdom you'll gain through this study won't just transform your life; it will overflow into the lives of those around you. As your understanding of God's wisdom deepens, you'll be better equipped to lead, encourage, and uplift others, reflecting Christ in every conversation, every decision, and every opportunity.

Journey of Transformation

This journey isn't just about becoming wiser for your sake—it's about becoming a beacon of wisdom for others, leading a life that points people back to God in every way.

Spiritual growth is a journey, not a destination. As you journey through this devotional, I encourage you to embrace the process of transformation that comes with pursuing wisdom. Every day offers a new opportunity to align your heart with God's heart, to shift your mindset from self-reliance to God-reliance.

Transformation doesn't happen overnight. Just as a plant needs water, sunlight, and good soil to grow, our hearts need daily nurturing through Scripture, prayer, and reflection. Over time, you will begin to see the fruit of wisdom take root in your life: in your relationships, your work, your decision-making, and your walk with God.

Remember, this journey is not about perfection; it's about progress. There will be times when you'll make mistakes or face challenges that make the road ahead seem unclear. But trust that God is with you every step of the way, using every moment to teach and grow you in wisdom.

HOW TO USE THIS DEVOTIONAL

This devotional is designed to guide you through three weeks of intentional study and reflection. Each day follows a structure aimed at helping you digest the truths of Scripture, reflect on their meaning, and apply them to your daily life.

- Scripture Reading: Each day begins with a key scripture that sets the foundation for the day's reflection.
- Example from Scripture: You'll read a biblical story or example that illustrates the day's theme. This brings the lesson to life, showing how wisdom was applied in real situations.
- Devotional Thought: These reflections are meant to provoke deep thought and personal application. Take time to journal your responses to capture your insights and growth.
- Questions for Reflection: Consider these prompts as a way to dive deeper into how the day's lesson applies to your life. This is where you'll start to see transformation as you wrestle with what it means to walk in wisdom.
- Daily Action Plan: Each day includes a practical action step to help you live out the principles you've learned. These actions will reinforce your understanding and encourage you to integrate godly wisdom into your daily decisions.

- Prayer: End each day with a time of prayer. Ask God to help you embrace His wisdom and guide you in living out His purpose for your life.

Welcome to this journey of discovering godly wisdom and making decisions that reflect the heart of Christ. I'm excited to walk with you through this transformational process, trusting that as we seek His wisdom together, God will guide us into deeper understanding and greater clarity.

WEEK 1
Embracing Godly Wisdom for Life's Decisions

Hey there, friend! Have you ever faced a decision so daunting that you found yourself frozen, unsure of which way to turn? You're not alone. We've all been there standing at a crossroads, unsure of which path aligns with God's will and afraid of making the wrong choice. I remember a time when I was in that exact position, overthinking every possible outcome. I prayed, I researched, I asked for advice, but still, I hesitated. Why? Because I hadn't yet embraced the kind of wisdom that comes from God—a wisdom that not only shows us what to do but helps us do it with peace and confidence.

In today's world, knowledge is literally at our fingertips. We've got AI assistants like Siri and Alexa answering our questions, Google providing instant solutions, and algorithms predicting what we want before we even know we need it. Whether it's mapping out the fastest route home, recommending products, or giving us the latest news update, technology seems to have an answer for everything. But here's the catch: knowledge isn't the same as wisdom.

AI can give us facts, but it can't give us the kind of wisdom that comes from a heart attuned to God. No matter how advanced technology becomes, it can never help us discern God's plan for our lives, guide us in making decisions that reflect His will, or provide us the peace that surpasses understanding (Philippians 4:7). The gap between knowledge and wisdom is one that no algorithm or machine can ever leap because wisdom comes from God, not just from information.

This week, we're diving deep into the heart of wisdom. We're going to explore what it truly means to live a life rooted in God's wisdom, not just worldly knowledge. Together, we'll unpack the biblical principles that guide us toward making godly decisions, no matter how big or small. Whether it's deciding on a career move, navigating relationships, or handling day-to-day challenges, godly wisdom is the key to walking the path that aligns with God's purpose for our lives.

Welcome to Week 1 of this journey into wisdom! This week, we'll lay the foundation for understanding how God equips us to make decisions that honor Him. We're going to discover that wisdom is not just about intellect or experience—it's about seeking God's guidance in every situation and trusting that He will direct our steps.

In a world filled with conflicting advice and endless options, it's easy to feel overwhelmed. But remember, we're not called to make decisions on our own. God promises to give us wisdom when we ask for it (James 1:5). So let's take this journey together, asking God to show us His way and embracing the wisdom that comes from a deep relationship with Him.

Key Themes

- Seeking God's Wisdom
- Trusting in God's Guidance
- Making Decisions with Confidence

Anchor Scripture

"If any of you lacks wisdom, you should ask God, who gives generously to all without finding fault, and it will be given to you."
—James 1:5

Reflection

As we begin this week, let's reflect on what it means to seek godly wisdom in our lives. Think about the areas where you've been relying on your own understanding and where you need to invite God's guidance. Take some time to meditate on God's promise to provide wisdom generously to those who ask. How would your decision-making process change if you fully trusted in His wisdom instead of your own?

DAY 1
MAKING GODLY DECISIONS THROUGH DISCERNMENT

Ever been faced with a decision so tough it felt like you were stuck at a fork in the road, unsure of which way to go? I've been there more times than I'd like to admit, and I'm sure you have too. One moment that sticks out was when I found myself choosing between two job offers. One was my dream job in a bustling city, offering excitement, prestige, and the chance to climb the corporate ladder. The other? A quieter, humbler role in a small town, aligning more with my core values but with far fewer accolades. It seemed like I was being pulled in two directions—head versus heart. As I wrestled with the decision, I did what I'd always done in the past: make a pros and cons list, talk to friends, and analyze the situation to death. But no matter how much I thought it through, I felt stuck.

It wasn't until I did something different—pausing and seeking God in prayer—that clarity began to surface. I realized discernment isn't just about making the "right" choice, but about making decisions that are aligned with God's will. It's less about what I want and more about where God is leading me. That was a game changer. Slowly but surely, I learned that discernment is a process—a relationship-based process of listening to God and trusting Him, even when the path ahead isn't clear.

This wasn't just about picking a job anymore; it was about learning to trust God with every part of my life, including the decisions I thought I could make on my own.

Role Models in Scripture

In 1 Kings 3:5-14, we meet Solomon, the young king of Israel, at the beginning of his reign. Can you imagine the pressure of ruling an entire nation, following in the footsteps of your father, King David? One night, God appeared to Solomon in a dream, offering him anything he desired. Now, think about that for a second—anything! Most of us might have asked for wealth, power, or long life. But Solomon? He didn't ask for those things. Instead, he asked for something much more profound discernment. He asked for the ability to distinguish right from wrong, to govern his people wisely, and to lead with justice.

God was so pleased with Solomon's request that He not only gave him wisdom but also blessed him with riches and honor. Solomon's story teaches us that godly wisdom isn't about getting ahead in life or accumulating more for ourselves. It's about asking God for the ability to make decisions that reflect His heart, His justice, and His love for others. Solomon's wisdom allowed him to navigate the complexities of leadership with grace, compassion, and clarity. His story challenges us to approach our own decisions, big and small, with the same mindset. Instead of asking, "What's best for me?" we should be asking, "What decision aligns with God's will and purposes for my life?"

Whether it's a job decision, a relationship question, or a choice about how to spend your time, God invites you to seek His wisdom, just as Solomon did. The decisions we make every day can either draw us closer to God's plan or pull us further away. Solomon's example reminds us that when we ask for discernment with a sincere heart, God will answer, guiding us toward the path that leads to righteousness and peace.

Scripture to Remember

"For the Lord gives wisdom; from his mouth come knowledge and understanding."
— Proverbs 2:6

"Trust in the Lord with all your heart and lean not on your own understanding; in all your ways submit to him, and he will make your paths straight."
— Proverbs 3:5-6

"If any of you lacks wisdom, you should ask God, who gives generously to all without finding fault, and it will be given to you."
— James 1:5

Consider This

Discernment is more than just making a choice between good and bad—it's about aligning every decision with God's will. The world often encourages us to trust in our own knowledge, to lean on logic or popular opinion, but godly wisdom comes from a place of surrender. It's about saying, "Lord, I trust You to lead me, even when I don't fully understand the path ahead." Like Solomon, when we ask for discernment with a heart that seeks God's guidance, we can rest in the assurance that He will provide the wisdom we need.

Questions for Reflection

1. Can you think of a time when you faced a difficult decision and struggled to trust God? How did you handle it?

_____

_____

_____

2. Where in your life right now do you need more discernment and godly wisdom?

_____

_____

_____

3. How does Solomon's example of asking for wisdom over personal gain inspire your approach to decision-making?

_____

_____

_____

Living Out Our Wisdom

This week, make a habit of pausing before making any decision, big or small. Instead of rushing to choose, take time to ask God for wisdom and discernment. Trust that He will guide you, even if the answer isn't immediate. Consider writing down the choices you're facing and inviting God into the decision-making process, praying for clarity and wisdom at every turn.

_____

_____

_____

_____

_____

_____

Building Deeper Connection to Faith

- Journaling Prompt: Reflect on a recent decision where you sought God's wisdom. How did He guide you? What did you learn through that process? Write about how you can continue to trust in God's wisdom for future decisions, even when the path isn't clear.
- Prayer: "Heavenly Father, I thank You for the gift of discernment. Help me to seek Your wisdom in all things, trusting in Your guidance above my own understanding. Like Solomon, may I desire wisdom that reflects Your heart, and may my decisions honor You in every way. Lead me, Lord, and teach me to walk in Your ways. Amen."

Solomon's request for wisdom teaches us that godly discernment is a gift that not only benefits us but those around us. As we learn to seek God's wisdom in every decision, we open the door for Him to lead us on a path of righteousness, peace, and purpose. Remember that God is always willing to guide us if we take the time to ask, listen, and trust in His perfect plan.

Tomorrow's Journey

Tomorrow, we will dive deeper into the consequences of ignoring wisdom, reflecting on how God uses both the positive and negative outcomes of our decisions to teach and guide us.

DAY 2
THE CONSEQUENCES OF
WISDOM IGNORED

There are moments in life when wisdom is like a quiet voice in the background—always there, offering guidance, but easy to ignore in the rush of our own desires and choices. Looking back, I realize how often I brushed aside that voice, thinking I knew better. We all do it at some point. For me, the lessons came slowly and painfully, as they often do when we ignore the wisdom that's right in front of us.

I still vividly remember the night when my mom's words began to make sense—though it took me a while to truly understand their weight. I was a teenager, living in the moment, focused on football, my friends, and more than a few reckless choices. That particular night, I came home way past curfew, expecting the usual scolding or perhaps silence from my parents. Instead, my mom was waiting, sitting at the kitchen table. She didn't yell or lecture. She just looked at me and said quietly, *"Eric, there's always a consequence."*

I brushed it off at the time, confident that I could dodge consequences the way I dodged mud puddles on the cross-country course. I believed consequences were negotiable, something you could charm your way out of or outrun if you were quick enough. But life doesn't work that way. The consequences caught up with me sooner than I expected—first, a disappointing grade on my report card from neglecting my studies, and later, a painful sprained ankle from pushing myself too hard in practice when I knew I should have rested.

The truth was always there, spoken through my mom, my coaches, even my teachers. Wisdom had been offered to me, not just in that moment but in countless others before and after. But I had ignored it. And as a result, I found myself facing consequences I could have easily avoided if I had just listened.

Consequences aren't always immediate. Sometimes they unfold gradually, catching us off guard after we've convinced ourselves we're invincible. But they always come. They remind us that wisdom—whether it's advice from a parent or insight from life experiences—isn't something to take lightly. When we ignore wisdom, we invite consequences into our lives, and the cost is often greater than we anticipated.

Role Models in Scripture King Solomon

King Solomon, renowned as the wisest man in history, was blessed with wisdom beyond measure. His wisdom is immortalized in the book of Proverbs, where he offers guidance on how to live a righteous, wise, and God-fearing life. His sayings emphasize the value of wisdom, discipline, and understanding, teaching us how to avoid pitfalls and live in harmony with God and others.

Yet, Solomon's life also serves as a cautionary tale. Despite possessing divine wisdom, he didn't always follow the principles he espoused. His early reign was marked by great achievements, including building the magnificent Temple in Jerusalem and leading Israel to a period of unprecedented peace and prosperity. However, as Solomon grew older, his decisions began to reflect compromise and disobedience to God's commands.

Solomon's downfall stemmed from his many political marriages, which he formed as alliances with foreign nations. While these marriages helped strengthen Israel politically, they had spiritual consequences. Solomon's wives brought with them the worship of foreign gods, and over time, Solomon allowed idol worship to spread in Israel, violating the very laws he was entrusted to uphold. This disobedience was a direct contradiction to the wisdom he had once embraced.

The consequence? After Solomon's death, the kingdom was torn apart, divided into two: the northern kingdom of Israel and the southern kingdom of Judah. The unity and peace Solomon had worked so hard to maintain were shattered because he chose to follow his own desires rather than God's wisdom. His legacy, once shining with glory, became tarnished by the idolatry and disobedience that followed him in his later years.

Solomon's life is a powerful reminder that wisdom, no matter how abundant, is only as valuable as the actions we take based on it. It's not enough to know what is right—we must choose to act on that knowledge, consistently and faithfully. Solomon's story warns us that even the wisest among us are vulnerable to pride, temptation, and compromise. His failure to heed his own wisdom serves as a sobering reminder that wisdom requires discipline, and the consequences of ignoring it can be profound and far-reaching.

For us today, Solomon's story encourages reflection: Are there areas in our lives where we know what is wise but fail to follow through? How can we ensure that we not only seek wisdom but also have the courage to live by it? Solomon's legacy, though flawed, offers a vital lesson: wisdom is a gift, but it requires vigilance and obedience to truly transform our lives.

Scripture to Remember

"Do not be wise in your own eyes;
fear the Lord and shun evil."
—Proverbs 3:7:

"If any of you lacks wisdom, you should ask God,
who gives generously to all without finding fault,
and it will be given to you."
—James 1:5:

Consider This

How many times have we known the wise thing to do but chose the opposite because it seemed inconvenient, unpopular, or simply less fun? God offers us wisdom through His Word, but it's up to us to act on it. Solomon's story shows us the danger of ignoring God's wisdom.

Questions for Reflection

1. What are some examples in your life where you've ignored wisdom?

_____

_____

_____

2. How did those choices affect you in the long run?

_____

_____

_____

3. In what areas of your life do you need to start asking for wisdom?

_____

_____

_____

Living Into Our Identity

To live out our identity in Christ means to choose wisdom daily, even when it's difficult. True wisdom leads us closer to God's will for our lives, helping us make decisions that reflect His heart.

_____

_____

_____

_____

_____

_____

Building Deeper Connection to Faith

- Journaling Prompt: Reflect on a time when you ignored wisdom and the consequences you faced. How might you approach a similar situation today with God's guidance?
- Prayer: "Lord, thank You for the gift of wisdom. Help me to choose it daily, even when it's hard or inconvenient. Guide my decisions so that they reflect Your love and grace. Amen."

Ignoring wisdom might feel convenient in the short term, but it always comes with a price. The quiet voice of wisdom is there to guide us, but we must choose to listen. Solomon's life reminds us that even with great wisdom, if we choose to ignore it, we invite unnecessary consequences into our lives. Take a moment to reflect on the areas in your life where you've brushed wisdom aside and ask God to help you embrace His guidance, even when it challenges your desires

Tomorrow's Journey

Tomorrow, we'll explore the wisdom found in humility, looking at how surrendering our pride opens the door for God to guide our lives in ways we never imagined.

DAY 3
THE WISDOM OF HUMILITY

There was a time in my early career when I thought I knew everything. I had just landed my first corporate job and believed I was on the fast track to success. I had the confidence, the drive, and a growing ego to match. My first big presentation was in front of senior leadership, and I was sure it would be a slam dunk. I walked into that room with my chest puffed up, completely unprepared for what came next: constructive criticism. They picked apart my proposal with precision, exposing gaps I hadn't even considered.

I walked out of that room humbled, realizing that true wisdom doesn't come from knowing everything—it comes from knowing that you don't. Humility is the doorway to wisdom.

Role Models in Scripture Moses

Moses was a man who didn't seek leadership, and yet God chose him to lead His people out of Egypt. Despite being chosen by God, Moses remained humble throughout his life, constantly seeking God's wisdom in leading the Israelites. When the weight of leadership became too much, he sought God's counsel, not relying on his own understanding.

Moses' humility was key to his wisdom. He knew that without God's guidance, he was powerless to lead. His life demonstrates that true wisdom comes from a humble heart willing to submit to God.

Scripture to Remember

"But those who hope in the Lord will renew their strength. They will soar on wings like eagles; they will run and not grow weary, they will walk and not be faint."
—Isaiah 40:31

"Wait for the Lord; be strong and take heart and wait for the Lord."
—Psalm 27:14

"The Lord is good to those who wait for Him, to the soul who seeks Him."
—Lamentations 3:25

Consider This

Humility is often misunderstood in today's world. We're taught to be confident, self-assured, and always in control. But biblical humility isn't about putting ourselves down—it's about lifting God up and acknowledging that His ways are higher than ours.

Questions for Reflection

1. How do you respond to constructive criticism or feedback?

    _____

    _____

    _____

2. In what areas of your life might pride be keeping you from true wisdom?

    _____

    _____

    _____

3. How can you cultivate humility in your daily decisions?

    _____

    _____

    _____

Living Into Our Identity

As children of God, we're called to walk in humility, trusting that His wisdom is greater than our own. This humility allows us to grow in wisdom and become more like Christ.

_____

_____

_____

_____

_____

_____

Building Deeper Connection to Faith

- Journaling Prompt: Reflect on a time when you had to humble yourself to gain wisdom. How did that experience change your perspective?
- Prayer: "Lord, teach me to walk in humility, recognizing that all wisdom comes from You. Help me to seek Your guidance in all areas of my life. Amen."

True wisdom requires humility. It's in recognizing our need for God and admitting that we don't have all the answers that we allow wisdom to grow. Solomon's request for wisdom was rooted in humility, and it's a powerful reminder that we must rely on God's guidance rather than our own understanding. Today, let's ask ourselves where we can set aside pride and allow God to lead us with His divine wisdom. Humility opens the door to growth and deeper wisdom.

Tomorrow's Journey

Tomorrow, we'll turn our attention to the power of listening. We'll consider how listening is essential to cultivating wisdom in our relationships and decision-making.

DAY 4
THE POWER OF LISTENING

In a family of five, with two teenage kids and three dogs, you quickly realize that everyone has something to say—and usually all at once! Whether it's the kids debating over who gets the last slice of pizza or the dogs barking at every squirrel in the yard, the noise never seems to stop. I used to pride myself on being a good listener, but one day, my daughter (with the brutal honesty only a teenager can offer) pointed out that I wasn't really listening at all—I was just waiting for my turn to speak. That was a wake-up call.

It hit me hard because, in that moment, I realized how much I'd been missing. I wasn't truly hearing the hearts of those around me, and worse yet, I wasn't leaving space for God to speak through them. True listening, I've learned, is much more than just hearing words—it's about being fully present, setting aside your own thoughts and agendas, and making room for wisdom to come from unexpected places.

Listening, I've come to understand, is not just a skill—it's an act of humility and a path to wisdom. When we slow down enough to truly listen—to others and to God—we open ourselves to deeper understanding and richer relationships.

Role Models in Scripture Samuel

Take Samuel, for example. When he was a young boy serving in the temple, God called out to him in the night. At first, Samuel didn't recognize the voice of God; he thought it was his mentor, Eli, calling him. But Samuel was attentive, and each time he heard the voice, he responded. It wasn't until Eli realized it was God speaking that Samuel understood what was happening. Yet, despite his initial confusion, Samuel's willingness to listen and be guided led him to become one of Israel's greatest prophets.

Samuel's life is a profound reminder of the power of listening. It wasn't his knowledge or experience that set him apart—it was his heart, open and ready to hear from God. His attentiveness not only allowed him to discern God's voice but also prepared him to lead a nation with wisdom and integrity.

Like Samuel, we too can miss God's voice in the noise of life. But when we take the time to quiet our hearts, listen with intention, and remain open to what God is saying through His Word and through others, we position ourselves to receive divine wisdom. Listening is more than just hearing words—it's an invitation to engage with God's direction for our lives.

Scripture to Remember

"Everyone should be quick to listen,
slow to speak and slow to become angry."
—James 1:19:

"To answer before listening—that is folly and shame."
—Proverbs 18:13:

Consider This

In today's fast-paced world, listening has become a lost art. We're so quick to give our opinion or defend our position that we miss the wisdom available to us when we simply listen.

Questions for Reflection

1. Do you listen to understand, or are you simply waiting for your turn to speak?

_____

_____

_____

2. How can you make space to hear God's voice in your life?

_____

_____

_____

3. Who in your life could you listen to more intentionally?

_____

_____

_____

Living Into Our Identity

Living out our identity in Christ means being willing to listen—to God and to others. It's through listening that we gain the wisdom we need to navigate life's challenges.

_____

_____

_____

_____

_____

_____

Building Deeper Connection to Faith

- Journaling Prompt: Think about a time when you didn't listen as well as you could have. How might that situation have turned out differently if you had listened more closely?
- Prayer: "Lord, give me ears to hear, not only Your voice but also the wisdom of those You've placed in my life. Help me to listen with humility and an open heart. Amen."

Listening is a practice that brings wisdom to life. When we truly listen—to God, to others, and to the wise counsel around us—we position ourselves to receive insight and understanding. Samuel's willingness to listen to God transformed his life and allowed him to lead with wisdom. Today, reflect on how you can become a better listener, tuning into the wisdom God is speaking to you through His Word and through the people He's placed in your life.

Tomorrow's Journey

Tomorrow, we'll discuss the importance of seeking counsel and how surrounding ourselves with wise voices helps us grow in faith and wisdom.

DAY 5
SEEKING COUNSEL

When I first started my publishing business, I was convinced I had it all figured out. I had years of experience under my belt, a strong vision for the future, and enough drive to push through any challenge. Or so I thought. I quickly found myself in over my head, juggling far too many responsibilities and, in the process, losing sight of the bigger picture. I was so focused on making sure everything was perfect that I forgot one critical thing: I couldn't do it all on my own.

One day, a mentor of mine—someone I deeply respected—pulled me aside and asked a question that changed everything. "Who's advising you?" he asked. The question seemed simple enough, but it hit me like a ton of bricks. In all my hustle, I hadn't stopped to seek wise counsel. I hadn't surrounded myself with people who could see the areas where I was blind, who could offer perspective and insight. I was trying to carry the entire load myself.

That moment shifted the trajectory of my business—and my life. I learned that wisdom doesn't mean doing it all alone. It means knowing when to seek help, when to lean on the counsel of those who have been where you want to go, and when to humbly accept advice that might challenge your pride. It's in those moments of humility that true growth happens.

Role Models in Scripture
King David and Nathan

One of the most powerful examples of seeking and accepting wise counsel can be found in the story of King David and the prophet Nathan. David, known as a man after God's own heart, was a powerful and influential leader, chosen by God to rule over Israel. But even David, despite his deep faith and devotion, made catastrophic mistakes. After committing adultery with Bathsheba and orchestrating the death of her husband, David spiraled into sin and deception. He was king, after all—who was there to hold him accountable?

Enter Nathan. God sent the prophet to confront David, not with a harsh condemnation, but with a carefully crafted story that would lead David to confront his own wrongdoing. Nathan's wisdom and approach gave David the space to see his actions clearly and to repent. David could have easily ignored Nathan or dismissed his rebuke—after all, he was the king. But instead, he listened. He allowed Nathan's words to penetrate his heart, and in doing so, he sought God's forgiveness.

David's willingness to accept wise counsel, even when it was difficult to hear, changed the course of his life. It's a lesson for all of us. No matter how strong we think we are, no matter how much we've achieved, we all need people in our lives who will speak the truth in love, who will challenge us to grow, and who will help us stay on the path of righteousness.

Scripture to Remember

"The way of fools seems right to them,
but the wise listen to advice."
—Proverbs 12:15

"Plans fail for lack of counsel,
but with many advisers they succeed."
—Proverbs 15:22:

Consider This

Who are the people speaking into your life? Do you have godly counsel that helps guide your decisions, or are you trying to navigate life on your own? Seeking wise counsel is a sign of strength, not weakness.

Questions for Reflection

1. Who is currently advising you in your spiritual journey?

_____

_____

_____

2. How do you respond to godly counsel when it challenges your own desires?

_____

_____

_____

3. How can you cultivate relationships with people who will offer you godly wisdom?

_____

_____

_____

Living Into Our Identity

As God's children, we're called to walk with others on this journey of faith. Seeking godly counsel helps us stay grounded in wisdom and accountable to God's truth.

Building Deeper Connection to Faith

- Journaling Prompt: Reflect on a time when you sought advice from someone wise. How did their counsel shape your decision or outcome?
- Prayer: "Lord, help me to seek wise counsel and to humbly receive it when it's offered. Surround me with people who will encourage and challenge me in my walk with You. Amen."

Seeking wise counsel is a key aspect of living a life led by God's wisdom. None of us are meant to make decisions in isolation, and even the wisest leaders, like King David, needed guidance from trusted voices. Solomon's life shows us that disregarding godly counsel can lead to disastrous consequences. Today, reflect on the people in your life whom you trust for wise counsel. Are you seeking their input when making important decisions? May we always be open to the wisdom of others as God works through them to guide our steps.

Tomorrow's Journey

Tomorrow, we'll conclude the week with reflections on seeking counsel and moving forward with God's wisdom guiding our steps as we build a foundation for making wise decisions.

WEEK 1 REFLECTION

As we come to the end of Week 1, take some time to reflect on what you have learned and how it has impacted your journey of making godly decisions. Use this space to jot down your thoughts, insights, and any actions you plan to take moving forward.

Reflection Questions

1. What key insights did I gain about wisdom this week?

_____

_____

_____

2. How has my understanding of godly wisdom changed or deepened?

_____

_____

_____

3. In what ways have I experienced God's presence and guidance during this week?

_____

_____

_____

4. What challenges did I face, and how did I overcome them?

_____

_____

_____

Personal Reflections

1. What specific steps can I take to continue strengthening my decision-making through godly wisdom?

_____

_____

_____

2. How can I incorporate the lessons learned into my daily life?

_____

_____

_____

3. Are there any areas where I still struggle with wisdom? How can I address them?

_____

_____

_____

Action Plan

List three practical actions you will take in the coming week to nurture your decision-making through godly wisdom.

1. _____

_____

2. _____

_____

3. _____

_____

PRAYER

Spend a few moments in prayer, asking God to help you integrate what you've learned into your daily life and to continue guiding you toward wisdom.

"Heavenly Father, thank You for the insights and growth I've experienced this week. Help me to carry these lessons into the coming days and to make decisions that reflect Your wisdom and love. Amen."

Additional Notes

Use this space to write down any additional thoughts, prayers, or reflections you have as you conclude this week.

_____

_____

_____

_____

_____

_____

_____

Preparing for Week 2
Living Wisely in Everyday Life

As we prepare to dive into Week 2 of this study, it's time to reflect on how the pursuit of wisdom can shape the practical aspects of our daily lives. While Week 1 laid the foundation of wisdom—its importance, its pursuit, and its relationship to our identity in Christ—Week 2 will challenge us to consider how wisdom guides us through everyday decisions, large and small.

We all make decisions every day that influence our relationships, work, finances, and even how we handle trials and conflict. Too often, we lean on our own understanding in these areas, thinking we know what's best or what's easiest, when God's wisdom often calls us to something deeper, something counter-cultural.

In the week ahead, we'll explore what it means to apply wisdom in everyday life. This means trusting in God's guidance rather than relying solely on our instincts, circumstances, or the advice of the world. It means choosing integrity in moments of temptation and seeking God's will above personal convenience.

As you prepare for this week, take a moment to pray and reflect on these questions:

1. Where in my life am I making decisions without seeking God's wisdom first?

_____

_____

_____

2. How might living wisely change the way I approach relationships, work, and even challenges?

_____

_____

_____

3. Am I willing to submit my choices to God, even when His path may seem more difficult than my own?

_____

_____

_____

Let's move forward, ready to live wisely in every corner of our lives, trusting that God's wisdom is perfect and leads to abundant life.

WEEK 2
Living Wisely in Everyday Life

In Week 2, we dive into the heart of wisdom—how it shows up in the everyday moments of our lives. While wisdom might sound like a grand concept, it's often seen in the small, daily decisions we make. Think of wisdom as your daily GPS, guiding you through your routines, conversations, and interactions, helping you stay aligned with God's plan.

We've all had moments where we wish we'd made better decisions—whether it was in handling conflict with a loved one, choosing how to spend our time, or dealing with stress at work. What if, instead of reacting in those moments, we paused and sought wisdom? That's the journey we're embarking on this week.

Living wisely isn't just about big life choices. It's about choosing how to respond when your teenager tests your patience or when a colleague at work pushes your buttons. It's about how you spend your time, how you manage your finances, and even how you speak to those around you. Wisdom is about letting God's truth influence every part of our daily lives. As we move through this week, we'll explore how wisdom guides us in our relationships, work, and even our speech. We'll look at the examples of biblical figures who displayed wisdom in both grand and simple moments and learn how we can apply those lessons today.

Remember, wisdom doesn't come overnight, nor does it come easily. But as we make the daily choice to live wisely, we align ourselves with God's will and grow in our relationship with Him. By the end of this week, we'll have practical tools to help us navigate life with wisdom, reflecting God's love and purpose in every decision.

Key Themes

- Wisdom in Relationships
- Wisdom in Stewardship
- Wisdom in Work and Career
- Wisdom in Trials
- Wisdom in Speech

Anchor Scripture

"Blessed are those who find wisdom,
those who gain understanding"
—Proverbs 3:13 –

Reflection

As we enter this week, consider how wisdom can transform the ordinary moments of your life. Reflect on how wisdom has shown up in your past decisions and how you can invite God's wisdom into the choices you make today.

DAY 1
WISDOM IN RELATIONSHIPS

When I was a teenager, I believed that relationships were easy if the other person understood me. If someone didn't get me, I thought, "Well, they're just not meant to be in my life." That narrow mindset left me with a series of shallow friendships. But as I got older, I began to realize something profound—true, lasting relationships aren't about finding people who think exactly like you. They're about navigating differences, offering grace, and, sometimes, giving without expecting anything in return. Much like a football team where each player has a unique role, relationships thrive when we understand that everyone brings something different to the table. Just as a quarterback needs a lineman to block for him, we need others to support us in ways we can't support ourselves.

Relationships test our patience, our capacity to forgive, and our ability to love beyond our own selfish desires. Whether it's friendships, family ties, or romantic relationships, wisdom calls us to look beyond our needs and see the bigger picture—relationships that honor God require humility, love, and a lot of grace. Like an athlete learning to trust his team, wisdom helps us navigate relationships so they grow deeper, stronger, and more life-giving.

Role Models in Scripture

The friendship between David and Jonathan is one of the most beautiful and wisdom-filled relationships in the Bible. Jonathan, the son of King Saul, should have been David's enemy. After all, David was anointed as the next king of Israel—taking the throne that should have belonged to Jonathan. But instead of jealousy or resentment, Jonathan showed incredible humility and love. He protected David, even risking his own life to warn him of Saul's murderous intentions. Their bond wasn't based on selfish gain or personal ambitions. Instead, it was grounded in mutual respect, loyalty, and, most importantly, a shared faith in God.

Jonathan's wisdom allowed him to see beyond his personal loss of the throne and embrace God's larger plan. He prioritized God's will over his desires, and his friendship with David became a model of what true, godly relationships should look like. Through Jonathan, we see that wisdom in relationships isn't about what we can gain but about how we can love others as God loves us—sacrificially and unconditionally.

Scriptures to Remember

"As iron sharpens iron, so one person sharpens another."
—Proverbs 27:17

"Two are better than one because they have a good return for their labor: If either of them falls down, one can help the other up."
—Ecclesiastes 4:9-10

"Greater love has no one than this: to lay down one's life for one's friends."
—John 15:13

Consider This

In your relationships, are you more focused on what you can get or what you can give? Wisdom teaches us that godly relationships thrive on selflessness, loyalty, and love, not personal gain.

Questions for Reflection

1. How do you practice wisdom in your closest relationships?

_____

_____

_____

2. What relationship challenges have you faced, and how could applying God's wisdom change the outcome?

_____

_____

_____

3. Where in your life do you need to demonstrate more humility and sacrificial love?

_____

_____

_____

Living Into Our Identity

As children of God, we are called to model His love in our relationships. Like Jonathan and David, godly wisdom helps us move past selfish ambitions and prioritize love, loyalty, and faithfulness. Through wisdom, we reflect God's grace in our interactions with others.

_____

_____

_____

_____

_____

_____

Building Deeper Connection to Faith

- Journaling Prompt: Reflect on a time when you struggled to put someone else's needs ahead of your own. How might approaching that relationship with wisdom and humility have changed things?
- Prayer: "Lord, help me to love others as You have loved me. Teach me to show wisdom in my relationships, putting others before myself and prioritizing Your will over my desires."

Godly wisdom in relationships requires us to move past selfishness and embrace humility, loyalty, and sacrificial love. Just as Jonathan protected David, true friends protect, uplift, and encourage one another in faith.

Tomorrow's Journey

Tomorrow, we'll reflect on how wisdom influences stewardship, not only in finances but also in how we manage the gifts and responsibilities God has entrusted to us.

DAY 2
WISDOM IN STEWARDSHIP

When I was a kid, my dad would always say, "Take care of what you've got, and it'll take care of you." At the time, I thought he was just talking about mowing the lawn or cleaning my room. But as I got older and started managing a family, finances, and my own businesses, I realized that stewardship is about so much more than just taking care of physical possessions. It's about managing all the resources God has entrusted to us—our time, our talents, our money, and even our relationships.

I've learned that how we manage what we're given reflects our wisdom and understanding of God's purpose for us. Whether it's making sure we're spending enough time with our kids, handling our finances responsibly, or even just taking care of our own health, wisdom calls us to be good stewards. It's a bit like being the captain of a sports team—when everyone plays their part and manages their responsibilities, the whole team functions better, and success follows.

Role Models in Scripture

One of the greatest examples of stewardship in the Bible is the story of Joseph. He wasn't just a man who knew how to handle resources; he was someone who knew how to handle them with wisdom, even in the worst of circumstances. Sold into slavery by his brothers, Joseph could have given up. But instead, he used his position in Potiphar's house to practice faithful stewardship. When falsely accused and imprisoned, he continued to show wisdom and integrity. Eventually, his ability to wisely manage Egypt's resources during a severe famine saved countless lives, including his own family.

Joseph's story teaches us that stewardship is not about how much we have but how well we manage what we've been given. Whether we are overseeing a nation's resources like Joseph or managing our household, wisdom calls us to be faithful with the little so we can be trusted with more.

Scriptures to Remember

"Whoever can be trusted with very little can also be trusted with much, and whoever is dishonest with very little will also be dishonest with much."
—Luke 16:10

"The wise store up choice food and olive oil, but fools gulp theirs down."
—Proverbs 21:20

"Each of you should use whatever gift you have received to serve others, as faithful stewards of God's grace in its various forms."
—1 Peter 4:10

Consider This

How are you stewarding the resources God has given you? Whether it's your finances, your time, or your relationships, wisdom calls us to manage everything with care and purpose.

Questions for Reflection

1. What areas of your life need better stewardship?

_____

_____

_____

2. How can you manage your resources—money, time, relationships—in a way that honors God?

_____

_____

_____

3. What practical steps can you take today to become a more faithful steward?

_____

_____

_____

Living Into Our Identity

As stewards of God's gifts, we are called to handle them with wisdom, whether big or small. Joseph's faithfulness in managing resources, even in hardship, is a powerful reminder that our stewardship reflects our trust in God's plan.

_____

_____

_____

_____

_____

_____

Building Deeper Connection to Faith

- Journaling Prompt: Make a list of the resources God has entrusted to you (time, money, relationships, talents). How can you improve your stewardship in these areas?
- Prayer: "Lord, help me to be a faithful steward of all You've given me. Teach me to manage my time, resources, and relationships wisely, always honoring You with what I've been entrusted."

Wisdom in stewardship means managing what God has given us with faithfulness and care, just as Joseph did in Egypt. Whether little or much, wisdom helps us honor God in every responsibility.

Tomorrow's Journey

Tomorrow, we'll shift our focus to how wisdom can transform our work and careers, guiding us in making ethical and faith-driven decisions in the workplace.

DAY 3
WISDOM IN WORK AND CAREER

Work has always been an essential part of my life, from my early days in corporate America to the various businesses I've run. One lesson I learned early on was that working hard wasn't enough. You could work the hardest longest, out last anyone, hours, but if you weren't working wisely, you'd still find yourself exhausted and, often, frustrated. I remember once taking on a project that seemed like the opportunity of a lifetime. The pay was excellent, and the challenge was enticing, but in my gut, something felt off. I ignored it, thinking I could push through, and what followed was months of stress, sleepless nights, and ultimately, the failure of the project. It was a hard lesson: hard work without wisdom leads to burnout, not success.

In our work and careers, wisdom helps us discern which opportunities to pursue, how to manage our time, and how to handle challenges with grace. It's not just about career success—it's about working in a way that honors God and reflects His purpose for us. Whether you're an employee, business owner, or stay-at-home parent, wisdom in work means aligning your efforts with God's plan, seeking His guidance in every task.

Role Models in Scripture

Nehemiah is one of the greatest examples of wisdom in work. Called to rebuild the walls of Jerusalem, he faced intense opposition. But rather than charging ahead without a plan, Nehemiah prayed for wisdom at every step. He carefully assessed the situation, gathered the right people, and approached the task with strategic planning. His wisdom wasn't just in working hard—it was in working smart. Nehemiah's wisdom allowed him to rally the people, overcome obstacles, and rebuild the walls of Jerusalem in just 52 days.

Nehemiah's story shows us that wisdom in work is about more than diligence; it's about seeking God's guidance, planning effectively, and persevering even when the odds seem stacked against us. Through his wisdom, Nehemiah not only rebuilt the physical walls of Jerusalem but also restored the people's faith and unity.

Scriptures to Remember

"Whatever you do, work at it with all your heart, as working for the Lord, not for human masters."
—Colossians 3:23

"Commit to the Lord whatever you do, and He will establish your plans."
—Proverbs 16:3

"Whatever your hand finds to do, do it with all your might."
—Ecclesiastes 9:10

Consider This

Are you working wisely, or are you just working hard? Wisdom in work means seeking God's direction in every task and aligning your efforts with His purpose.

Questions for Reflection

1. How can you invite God's wisdom into your work or career?

   _____

   _____

   _____

2. Are there tasks or responsibilities where you've been working harder rather than wiser?

   _____

   _____

   _____

3. How can you approach your daily work with a mindset that honors God?

   _____

   _____

   _____

Living Into Our Identity

As followers of Christ, we're called to work with excellence, not just for our own success but as a reflection of God's kingdom. Wisdom in work reminds us that our efforts, no matter how small or large, should be dedicated to God's glory.

_____

_____

_____

_____

_____

_____

Building Deeper Connection to Faith

- Journaling Prompt: Think about a time when you worked hard but felt burnt out. How could inviting God's wisdom into that situation have changed the outcome?
- Prayer: "Lord, help me to work with wisdom and not just effort. Teach me to seek Your guidance in every task and to work in a way that honors You."

Wisdom in work is about aligning your efforts with God's purpose, seeking His guidance, and trusting Him to establish your steps. Like Nehemiah, we can accomplish great things when we work wisely and rely on God's wisdom.

Tomorrow's Journey

Tomorrow, we'll explore how wisdom helps us navigate life's trials, offering a sense of peace and trust in God's greater plan during difficult times.

DAY 4
WISDOM IN TRIALS

We've all been through difficult times—those seasons where nothing seems to go right. I remember when one of my businesses was struggling. It felt like no matter what I did, it wasn't enough to keep things afloat. My immediate reaction was to try to fix everything myself, but the more I tried, the worse things seemed to get. Eventually, I reached a breaking point and realized that wisdom in trials isn't about knowing all the answers—it's about knowing when to trust God and when to ask for help.

Trials test our faith, patience, and wisdom. They can either break us or strengthen us, depending on how we approach them. Wisdom in trials isn't about having all the solutions; it's about leaning into God's guidance, trusting Him through the storm, and seeking the lessons He's trying to teach us along the way.

Role Models in Scripture

Job's story is perhaps the most well-known example of wisdom in trials. A righteous man who loved God, Job lost everything—his family, his wealth, and his health. But through it all, he remained faithful. Job didn't have all the answers. In fact, he questioned God's reasons for allowing such suffering. But his wisdom was in his persistence—he never stopped seeking God, even when he didn't understand.

Job's wisdom in trials wasn't about having an easy solution; it was about trusting God, even when everything seemed hopeless. His story reminds us that wisdom in trials means enduring with faith, even when we don't see the way forward. It's about holding on to the truth that God is good, even in the midst of hardship.

Scriptures to Remember

"Consider it pure joy, my brothers and sisters, whenever you face trials of many kinds, because you know that the testing of your faith produces perseverance."
—James 1:2-4

"Not only so, but we also glory in our sufferings, because we know that suffering produces perseverance; perseverance, character; and character, hope."
—Romans 5:3-4

"But those who hope in the Lord will renew their strength. They will soar on wings like eagles; they will run and not grow weary, they will walk and not be faint."
—Isaiah 40:31

Consider This

How do you respond to trials in your life? Wisdom calls us to trust God's process, even when we don't understand the outcome.

Questions for Reflection

1. How has a recent trial tested your faith?

_____

_____

_____

2. In what ways can you seek God's wisdom in difficult situations rather than relying on your own understanding?

_____

_____

_____

3. What lessons might God be teaching you through your current trials?

_____

_____

_____

Living Into Our Identity

As children of God, we're called to persevere through trials with faith and trust in God's goodness. Wisdom helps us see beyond the immediate pain to the bigger picture of God's purpose.

_____

_____

_____

_____

_____

Building Deeper Connection to Faith

- Journaling Prompt: Think about a recent trial. How has your faith been tested? How can wisdom help you navigate this difficult time?
- Prayer: "Lord, I trust You in the trials of life. Give me the wisdom to see Your hand at work, even when I don't understand the reasons."

Wisdom in trials isn't about having all the answers; it's about trusting God through the storm. Like Job, we can hold on to faith, knowing that God is working all things for our good.

Tomorrow's Journey

Tomorrow, we'll conclude the week by looking at how wisdom guides our speech, helping us speak life and encouragement into others and reflect God's love in all conversations.

DAY 5
WISDOM IN SPEECH

When I was younger, I thought that the more you talked, the more people would listen. I had this idea that if I just kept explaining myself, people would eventually get my point. But as I've gotten older, I've learned the hard way that wisdom in speech often means knowing when to stay silent. I can remember a time when I said something in the heat of the moment—words I didn't really mean—that hurt a close friend deeply. Even though I apologized, the damage was done. It was a painful lesson in the power of words and the need for wisdom in how we use them.

Our words have the power to build up or tear down, to encourage or discourage. Wisdom in speech means choosing our words carefully, thinking before we speak, and using our speech to reflect God's love. In a world filled with noise and constant talking, wisdom teaches us the value of silence, listening, and speaking truth with grace. Even recently I relearned the lesson that my role is not always to jump in and teach from my position of wisdom but to create the silent space for others to discover their own wisdom in their words.

Role Models in Scripture

James, the brother of Jesus, is one of the most direct and powerful voices in the New Testament when it comes to the importance of our speech. Although he did not initially believe in Jesus during His ministry, James eventually became a devoted follower and leader of the early church. His epistle is full of practical wisdom on living out faith, with a special focus on how our words reflect our hearts and can influence our lives and the lives of those around us.

In his letter, James compares the tongue to a small rudder that steers a large ship, warning that even though the tongue is a small part of the body, it can cause great destruction. He uses vivid imagery to describe the tongue as a spark that can set a forest ablaze, emphasizing how words, though seemingly insignificant, have immense power to build up or tear down (James 3:5-6). He encourages believers to be quick to listen, slow to speak, and slow to anger (James 1:19), understanding that wisdom is not just in what we say, but in the timing and intention behind our words.

James' teaching challenges us to recognize the weight of our speech. Our words are not neutral; they either bring life or death, healing or hurt, blessing or curse. His wisdom urges us to be intentional with every word we speak, reflecting the heart of God in our conversations and interactions. James understood firsthand how deeply words can impact individuals and communities, especially in a world filled with noise and division. His insights call us to speak thoughtfully, always aiming to edify others and promote peace.

Scriptures to Remember

"The tongue has the power of life and death,
and those who love it will eat its fruit."
—Proverbs 18:21

"Likewise, the tongue is a small part of the body, but it
makes great boasts. Consider what a great forest is set on
fire by a small spark. The tongue also is a fire, a world of
evil among the parts of the body."
—James 3:5-6

"A gentle answer turns away wrath,
but a harsh word stirs up anger."
—Proverbs 15:1

Consider This

How often do you speak without thinking? Wisdom in speech calls us to think before we speak and to use our words to encourage, uplift, and reflect God's love.

Questions for Reflection

1. In what areas of your life do you need more wisdom in your speech?

_____

_____

_____

2. How can you use your words to build others up and reflect God's love?

_____

_____

_____

3. What practical steps can you take to be more intentional with your speech?

_____

_____

_____

Living Into Our Identity

As believers, our words are a reflection of our faith. Wisdom in speech means using our words to bring life, encouragement, and grace to those around us, just as Christ's words bring life to us.

_____

_____

_____

_____

_____

_____

Building Deeper Connection to Faith

*   Journaling Prompt: Think about a time when your words caused harm. How can you seek wisdom in future conversations to reflect God's love?

- Prayer: "Lord, help me to use my words wisely. Let my speech be filled with grace, truth, and encouragement, always reflecting Your love to others."

Wisdom in speech calls us not only to think carefully before we speak but to recognize the profound influence our words can have on those around us. Our speech has the power to either lift others up or tear them down, to build bridges of understanding or create walls of division. As followers of Christ, we are called to use our words as instruments of grace, speaking life, encouragement, and truth into every conversation. When we align our speech with God's love and truth, we reflect His character and demonstrate the transformative power of His wisdom at work in us.

Tomorrow's Journey

Tomorrow, we'll start Week 3 by delving into how wisdom and faith are deeply connected, and how walking in faith brings deeper understanding of God's wisdom.

WEEK 2 REFLECTION

As we come to the end of Week 2, take some time to reflect on the lessons learned about living wisely in everyday life. Wisdom isn't just about big decisions—it's about how we live out our faith in the small, daily moments.

Reflection Questions

1. How has your understanding of wisdom in relationships, work, or speech deepened this week?

_____

_____

_____

2. In what areas of your life do you need to invite more of God's wisdom?

_____

_____

_____

3. What practical steps can you take to apply wisdom in your daily decisions moving forward?

_____

_____

_____

Personal Reflections

1. How have you seen wisdom transform your relationships or work life?

_____

_____

_____

2. What challenges did you face this week, and how did wisdom help you overcome them?

_____

_____

_____

3. How can you continue to seek wisdom in the small, everyday moments of life?

_____

_____

_____

Action Plan

List three practical actions you will take to apply wisdom in your daily life:

1. _____

_____

2. _____

_____

3. _____

_____

PRAYER

Spend a few moments in prayer, asking God to help you integrate what you've learned into your daily life and to continue guiding you on your faith journey.

"Lord, thank You for the wisdom You've given me this week. Help me to continue seeking Your guidance in my relationships, work, and speech. May Your wisdom shape every decision I make, and may I always live in a way that honors You. Amen."

Additional Notes

Use this space to write down any additional thoughts, prayers, or reflections you have as you conclude this week.

Preparing for Week 3 Wisdom and Faith

As we prepare to enter Week 3, we shift our focus from practical decision-making to the beautiful relationship between wisdom and faith. Last week, we explored how wisdom affects our daily decisions—how it informs our work, relationships, and even how we navigate conflict. Now, it's time to look deeper into how wisdom and faith work hand-in-hand.

In the week ahead, we'll explore how faith and wisdom are not opposing forces but rather companions on our spiritual journey. True wisdom is deeply rooted in trusting God, even when circumstances seem uncertain or challenging. Wisdom calls us to have patience, to wait on God's timing, and to surrender our fears, knowing that His ways are always higher than ours.

This week will invite you to reflect on what it means to walk in both faith and wisdom, allowing God to guide your steps with confidence and clarity. The journey of faith often involves moments of waiting, perseverance, and the courage to choose trust over fear. Wisdom leads us to deeper faith as we recognize that God's wisdom transcends human understanding, and it is through this trust that we grow closer to Him.

As you prepare for this week, take some time to ask yourself:

1. How do I respond when God's wisdom calls me to wait or trust in the unseen?

---

2. Where in my life do I need to embrace both wisdom and faith, rather than leaning solely on my own understanding?

---

3. Am I willing to trust God's wisdom even when it challenges my comfort or expectations?

_____

_____

_____

Let's prepare our hearts and minds to grow in both wisdom and faith, walking confidently with God every step of the way.

WEEK 3
Wisdom and Faith

In Week 3, we turn our focus to the deep, intertwined connection between wisdom and faith. Wisdom isn't merely about making smart decisions; it's about trusting that God's plan for us is greater than anything we could devise on our own. Faith, on the other hand, requires us to surrender our limited understanding, trusting that God's perfect wisdom is guiding us through even the most uncertain of times.

We often find ourselves at crossroads in life where the path ahead isn't clear. It's in these moments that wisdom and faith converge. Wisdom helps us discern the steps we should take, while faith empowers us to trust God's timing and direction, even when the road seems unclear or daunting. Faith asks us to release control, while wisdom anchors us in the knowledge that God's ways are higher than our own.

Throughout this week, we will explore powerful stories from Scripture where wisdom and faith were put to the test—stories of people who faced great challenges and uncertainties yet chose to trust God's wisdom over their own understanding. As we delve into these stories, we'll be reminded that walking in faith doesn't always mean understanding every step. Sometimes, it's about trusting in God's infinite wisdom, knowing He sees what we cannot.

When life's pressures mount and we are tempted to rely on our own instincts, faith reminds us that God is always working for our good. Wisdom teaches us to pause, to seek His counsel, and to move forward with trust. As we walk through this week, we will deepen our understanding of how to live with both wisdom and faith, trusting God's plan even when we can't see the whole picture.

Key Themes

- Trusting God's Plan
- Walking in Faith and Wisdom
- Wisdom in Patience and Waiting
- Faith Over Fear
- Embracing Godly Wisdom

Anchor Scripture

*"The fear of the Lord is the beginning of wisdom,
and knowledge of the Holy One is understanding."*
—Proverbs 9:10

Reflection

As we enter this week, consider how wisdom and faith have played out in your life so far. Have there been moments where you struggled to trust God's wisdom? Or times when you relied more on your own understanding rather than surrendering to God's plan?

Spend a few moments reflecting on the following

1. Where in your life do you find it difficult to trust God's wisdom?

_____

_____

_____

2. Are there areas where you rely too much on your own understanding and need to surrender control to God?

_____

_____

_____

3. How has your faith grown in times when you've chosen to follow God's wisdom over your own desires or plans?

_____

_____

_____

Let this week be a time of deep trust and surrender, as you reflect on God's unwavering wisdom and how it shapes every aspect of your faith journey.

DAY 1
TRUSTING GOD'S PLAN

Trusting God's plan is one of the most difficult aspects of faith. It's natural for us to want control, to map out our lives and know what's coming next. I've faced moments in my life where I tried to do everything by my plan. Early in my career, I had a vision for where I wanted to go, and I thought I had the wisdom to get there. I made all the right moves, or so I thought, but things didn't turn out as I had expected. A business deal that looked promising fell apart, leaving me questioning everything. I thought I had used wisdom, weighing the pros and cons, consulting with advisors, and working out every detail. But one thing was missing—I hadn't asked God for His wisdom or guidance.

The disappointment from that failed venture taught me a critical lesson: Trusting God's plan sometimes means surrendering our own. I had been so focused on my own agenda that I hadn't paused to consider what God wanted for me. After reflecting on that experience, I realized that wisdom and faith go hand in hand. It's not enough to plan—we need to trust God with those plans. Wisdom teaches us to acknowledge that His plan is higher than ours, even when it doesn't make sense.

Role Models in Scripture

One of the most powerful biblical examples of trusting God's plan is Joseph's story. Joseph was sold into slavery by his brothers, unjustly imprisoned, and seemingly forgotten for years. Yet through it all, Joseph trusted that God was still at work in his life. In Genesis 50:20, Joseph tells his brothers, "*You intended to harm me, but God intended it for good to accomplish what is now being done, the saving of many lives.*"

Joseph's story reminds us that trusting God's plan often requires enduring seasons of hardship and waiting. In his early years, Joseph could not have predicted that he would become a ruler in Egypt, saving nations from famine. But God was working behind the scenes, using even the difficult circumstances to fulfill His greater purpose.

Joseph's unwavering trust in God's plan is a model for us today. No matter what we face—disappointments, setbacks, or unexpected detours—God's wisdom is guiding us. When we choose to trust His plan, even when it looks different from our own, we position ourselves to experience His ultimate goodness.

Scriptures to Remember

"*In their hearts humans plan their course,
but the Lord establishes their steps.*"
—Proverbs 16:9

"*And we know that in all things God works for the good of those who love Him, who have been called according to His purpose.*"
—Romans 8:28

"For I know the plans I have for you," declares the Lord, "plans to prosper you and not to harm you, plans to give you hope and a future."
—Jeremiah 29:11

Consider This

Are you trying to hold onto control, or are you willing to trust God's plan? Reflect on how Joseph trusted God even in the darkest times of his life. Can you find the faith to believe that God is working for your good, even when you don't understand His plan?

Questions for Reflection

1. What area of your life are you struggling to trust God with right now?

    _____

    _____

    _____

2. How does Joseph's story encourage you to trust God's plan, even in difficult circumstances?

    _____

    _____

    _____

3. What practical steps can you take to surrender control and trust God's wisdom?

    _____

    _____

    _____

Living Into Our Identity

As children of God, we are called to live in faith, trusting that God's plans for us are good. When we place our trust in His wisdom rather than our own, we align ourselves with His greater purpose. Just like Joseph, we may not always understand why we face certain trials, but we can rest assured that God is working all things for our good.

_____

_____

_____

_____

_____

_____

Building Deeper Connection to Faith

- Journaling Prompt: Reflect on a time in your life when things didn't go according to your plan. How did you respond, and how might you respond differently if you trusted God's plan more fully?
- Prayer: "Heavenly Father, I confess that I sometimes try to control my life and make decisions without seeking Your wisdom. Help me to trust Your plan for my life, even when I don't understand it. Give me the faith to surrender my will to Yours and to trust that You are working all things for my good. Amen."

Trusting God's plan requires faith and wisdom. Like Joseph, we may face seasons of difficulty and uncertainty, but we can trust that God's wisdom is guiding us to a greater purpose.

Tomorrow's Journey

Tomorrow, we'll delve into how wisdom and faith walk hand in hand, and how trusting God's wisdom can guide us even in moments of uncertainty.

DAY 2
WALKING IN FAITH
AND WISDOM

Have you ever walked a tightrope, or maybe you've watched someone else do it? There's a delicate balance required—one misstep, and it's easy to lose your footing. Walking in faith and wisdom is similar. It requires careful balance between trusting God and applying the wisdom He gives us. Faith and wisdom are not mutually exclusive; they work together, guiding us through life's challenges.

I remember a season in my life when I tried to walk in faith, but I wasn't using wisdom. I thought I could take on a new business venture without really seeking God's direction. You see I had faith that everything would work out because I believed God was with me, after all anytime someone tried to offer me cautionary advice I would simply say "don't worry Gods got it" but I hadn't taken the time to seek His wisdom for the decision. As you can imagine, things didn't go as planned, and I ended up frustrated and disheartened. I'll save you the long drama filled pity party victim me story. The story I told myself for far too long. When I final got real with myself I was able to see. That experience taught me that faith and wisdom are two sides of the same coin.

Blind faith is not real faith at best it's foolish faith. And you know what they say about a fool and his folly. (Proverbs 26:4-5). You need both to navigate life's challenges effectively.

Role Models in Scripture

Abraham's journey offers a profound example of how faith and wisdom are intertwined. In Genesis 12, God called Abraham to leave everything familiar—his country, his people, and his father's household—and set out for an unknown land that God would eventually show him. This wasn't a journey with clear directions or guarantees, but Abraham chose to trust in God's wisdom. Imagine the uncertainty he must have felt, yet his faith compelled him to move forward, even when the destination was unclear.

Hebrews 11:8 reminds us of this faith when it says, "*By faith Abraham, when called to go to a place he would later receive as his inheritance, obeyed and went, even though he did not know where he was going.*" Abraham's trust wasn't based on seeing the full picture; it was grounded in the understanding that God's wisdom far exceeded his own. He relied on God to lead the way, trusting that the plan set before him was far greater than any plan he could design for himself.

What stands out about Abraham is that his faith was not blind. It was deeply rooted in wisdom—the kind of wisdom that comes from knowing who God is and believing in His promises. Abraham understood that God's wisdom was the key to his journey's success. He followed God's leading, one step at a time, trusting that even if he couldn't see the full path, God had already mapped out every detail.

Because of his faith and obedience, God fulfilled His promise to Abraham, making him the father of many nations. Abraham's story reminds us that when we allow faith and wisdom to work hand in hand, we can step into the unknown with confidence, knowing that God will guide our steps toward His ultimate purpose.

Scriptures to Remember

"Trust in the Lord with all your heart and lean not on your own understanding; in all your ways submit to Him, and He will make your paths straight."
—Proverbs 3:5-6

"For we live by faith, not by sight."
—2 Corinthians 5:7

"Now faith is confidence in what we hope for and assurance about what we do not see."
—Hebrews 11:1

Consider This

Are you walking in faith and wisdom, or are you trying to separate the two? God calls us to trust Him and seek His wisdom in every step we take. How can you begin to bring more balance between faith and wisdom in your life?

Questions for Reflection

1. How can you better incorporate both faith and wisdom into your decision-making?

_____

_____

_____

2. In what areas of your life are you relying too much on your own understanding, rather than trusting God's wisdom?

_____

_____

_____

3. How does Abraham's story inspire you to step out in faith, trusting that God will provide the wisdom you need?

_____

_____

_____

Living Into Our Identity

As believers, our identity is rooted in faith and wisdom. Walking in faith means trusting God with the unknown, while wisdom guides us in making decisions that honor Him. Like Abraham, we are called to step out in faith, trusting that God will guide us every step of the way.

_____

_____

_____

_____

_____

_____

Building Deeper Connection to Faith

- Journaling Prompt: Think about a recent decision you made. How did faith and wisdom play a role in that decision? How could you have trusted God more fully?
- Prayer: "Lord, help me to walk in faith and wisdom. Guide my steps and give me the courage to trust You, even when I don't see the way ahead. Teach me to lean on Your wisdom in all areas of my life. Amen."

Walking in faith and wisdom requires balance. Like Abraham, we are called to trust God's wisdom and step out in faith, knowing that He will guide our steps.

Tomorrow's Journey

Tomorrow, we'll explore the virtue of patience and how waiting on God's timing requires both faith and wisdom in the face of life's challenges.

DAY 3
WISDOM IN PATIENCE AND WAITING

Waiting is one of the hardest things to do, especially in our fast-paced, instant-gratification world. If I'm being honest, I've never been good at waiting. Whether it's waiting in line at the grocery store or waiting for an important business deal to finalize, I've always found myself growing impatient. My family quickly learned that when Dad says "10 minutes," he really means more like 5. And don't even get me started on waiting and being late—two things that, in my book, are simply not allowed. Even if the earth were crashing into the sun, I'd probably still insist we get there early!

But life has a funny way of humbling you. Over the years, I've learned that there's wisdom to be found in waiting—or maybe, I've just been worn down a bit in my old age! I've come to understand that wisdom and patience are closely connected, and the waiting season isn't wasted time; it's where growth happens.

There was a time in my career when I was waiting on a critical contract to be finalized. I had done everything in my power to push it forward, but no matter what I tried, I felt like I was stuck in limbo. Each day, I would wake up anxious, wondering when I'd finally receive that call confirming the deal. As the weeks turned into months, frustration crept in. I wanted to control the timeline, to make things happen faster.

But during that long waiting period, I began to realize something. God wasn't keeping the deal from happening—He was teaching me a valuable lesson in patience. Instead of constantly fretting and trying to rush the process, I began to pray for wisdom in the waiting. I learned that there's something sacred about waiting on God's timing, rather than forcing things on my own. As I trusted Him more, the anxiety slowly faded, and peace took its place. Waiting wasn't about inaction; it was about trusting that God's timing is always perfect, even when we can't see it.

Role Models in Scripture

David's life is a powerful example of wisdom in waiting. As a young boy, David was anointed to be the next king of Israel, but it took years for that promise to come to fruition. During those years, David didn't just wait idly—he faced trials, persecution, and even moments where it seemed like taking matters into his own hands might make more sense.

In one of the most telling moments of David's life, we find him in a cave, hiding from King Saul, who was relentlessly hunting him down. Saul entered the very cave where David was hiding, completely unaware that his enemy was within striking distance. David's men urged him to seize the moment and kill Saul, insisting that this was the perfect opportunity to fulfill his destiny as king.

But David saw it differently. Rather than taking vengeance or forcing God's promise, he chose to wait on God's timing. He recognized that stepping ahead of God's plan, even if it seemed like the perfect moment, would not honor the Lord. As he told his men, "*The Lord forbid that I should do such a thing to my master, the Lord's anointed"* (1 Samuel 24:6).

It would have been so easy for David to rationalize taking Saul's life. He could have ended years of running and hiding, claimed the throne, and fulfilled what seemed like a divinely appointed moment. But David exercised patience and wisdom, trusting that God's plan and timing were better than anything he could orchestrate on his own.

David's story shows us the strength it takes to wait on God, even when the path forward seems clear to us. It's a reminder that wisdom is about trusting God's timing, not rushing ahead. In the same way, when we are faced with seasons of waiting, we must trust that God is working behind the scenes, preparing us for what's to come, just as He was preparing David. Through our waiting, God shapes our character and our trust in Him.

Scriptures to Remember

"But those who hope in the Lord will renew their strength. They will soar on wings like eagles; they will run and not grow weary, they will walk and not be faint."
—Isaiah 40:31

"Wait for the Lord; be strong and take heart and wait for the Lord."
—Psalm 27:14

"The Lord is good to those who wait for Him, to the soul who seeks Him."
—Lamentations 3:25

Consider This

Are you in a season of waiting? How can you use this time to seek God's wisdom and trust His timing? Reflect on how David waited patiently for God to fulfill His promises. Are you willing to trust God in the same way?

Questions for Reflection

1. How has impatience affected your decisions in the past?

_____

_____

_____

2. In what area of your life are you waiting for God's timing?

_____

_____

_____

3. How does David's story encourage you to trust God in your season of waiting?

_____

_____

_____

Living Into Our Identity

As children of God, we are called to wait on His perfect timing. In the waiting, we learn to trust His wisdom and surrender our need for control. Like David, we can rest in the knowledge that God will fulfill His promises in His time.

_____

_____

_____

_____

_____

_____

Building Deeper Connection to Faith

- Journaling Prompt: Reflect on a time when you had to wait for something important. How did you handle the waiting, and how might you handle it differently now, with wisdom and faith?
- Prayer: "Lord, teach me to wait on Your timing. Help me to trust that You are working, even when I can't see the full picture. Give me the wisdom to be patient and the faith to trust You completely. Amen."

Wisdom in waiting means trusting God's timing. Like David, we are called to wait patiently, knowing that God's promises will be fulfilled.

Tomorrow's Journey

Tomorrow, we'll reflect on how to cultivate both wisdom and faith through perseverance, even in the midst of doubt and delay.

DAY 4
FAITH OVER FEAR

Fear is a powerful emotion. It can creep into our minds and paralyze us, keeping us from stepping into God's plans for our lives. I've faced many moments of fear in my life—whether it was fear of failure in my career, fear of financial uncertainty, or fear of making the wrong decision in pivotal moments. The truth is, fear can cloud our judgment and distort our ability to see the bigger picture of what God has in store. But through years of trial and error, I've learned that faith in God's wisdom is the antidote to fear.

There was a time when I had to make a major career decision that would significantly alter my path. The uncertainty was overwhelming, and fear almost stopped me in my tracks. I remember being afraid of the unknown, of the risks, of the possibility of making the wrong choice and regretting it later. The fear of failure weighed heavily on me. But as I prayed and sought God's wisdom, I began to realize that my faith had to be stronger than my fear.

In that pivotal moment, I chose to step out in faith, trusting that God's wisdom would guide me, even when the path wasn't clear. It wasn't easy, and the fear didn't vanish overnight. But what I discovered was that each step of faith I took was met with God's provision, reassurance, and a growing sense of confidence in His plan. I realized that fear will always be present, but faith in God's wisdom is what empowers us to move forward despite it.

Role Models in Scripture

One of the most well-known stories of faith overcoming fear is found in the life of Joshua. After the death of Moses, Joshua was entrusted with the enormous responsibility of leading the Israelites into the Promised Land. This wasn't just a promotion—it was a daunting task that carried the weight of an entire nation's future. Joshua had every reason to feel overwhelmed and afraid. The enemies in the land were strong, the challenges ahead seemed insurmountable, and the legacy of Moses cast a long shadow. Fear could have easily consumed him.

But God's words to Joshua were clear and direct: "Be strong and courageous. Do not be afraid; do not be discouraged, for the Lord your God will be with you wherever you go" (Joshua 1:9). This wasn't just a command; it was a divine promise that God's presence would be with Joshua every step of the way. God didn't promise an easy journey, but He promised His wisdom and guidance. Joshua's strength didn't come from his own abilities or strategies; it came from his trust in God's promises.

Joshua's story teaches us a powerful lesson about overcoming fear. He could have let the fear of failure, opposition, and the unknown hold him back. But instead, he chose to place his faith in God's wisdom, stepping into the unknown with courage and trust. Just as Joshua led the Israelites into the Promised Land by relying on God's guidance, we too are called to trust God's wisdom over our fears. Faith doesn't eliminate fear, but it empowers us to move forward, knowing that God is with us, guiding our steps and making a way.

Scriptures to Remember

"So do not fear, for I am with you; do not be dismayed,
for I am your God. I will strengthen you and help you;
I will uphold you with my righteous right hand."
—Isaiah 41:10

"When I am afraid, I put my trust in You. In God,
whose word I praise—in God I trust and am not afraid.
What can mere mortals do to me?"
—Psalm 56:3-4

"For the Spirit God gave us does not make us timid,
but gives us power, love and self-discipline."
—2 Timothy 1:7

Consider This

What fears are holding you back from fully trusting God? How can you choose faith over fear in your decisions? Reflect on Joshua's courage to move forward, despite the fear of the unknown.

Questions for Reflection

1. What fears are keeping you from stepping into God's plan for your life?

_____

_____

_____

2. How can you strengthen your faith to overcome those fears?

_____

_____

_____

3. How does Joshua's story encourage you to choose faith over fear?

_____

_____

_____

Living Into Our Identity

As believers, we are called to live by faith, not fear. God's wisdom and presence are with us, just as they were with Joshua. When we trust in God's wisdom, we can step out in faith, knowing that He will guide and protect us.

_____

_____

_____

_____

_____

_____

Building Deeper Connection to Faith

- Journaling Prompt: Write about a time when fear almost stopped you from stepping into God's plan. How did you overcome that fear, or how might you approach it differently now, with faith and wisdom?

- Prayer: "Lord, help me to choose faith over fear. Remind me that Your wisdom is greater than my fears, and that You are with me every step of the way. Give me the courage to trust You fully and to step into the plans You have for me. Amen."

Choosing faith over fear requires trust in God's wisdom. Like Joshua, we are called to be strong and courageous, knowing that God is with us.

Tomorrow's Journey

Tomorrow, we'll focus on how wisdom and trust in God's timing bring peace in the face of adversity. We'll learn to release control and surrender our desires to His perfect will.

DAY 5
EMBRACING GODLY
WISDOM

Wisdom is not something we acquire overnight—it's something we grow into, step by step, often through experiences that challenge us and push us to seek God's guidance. I've come to learn that embracing godly wisdom requires three essential things: humility, patience, and a deep willingness to be taught by the Lord. There have been countless times in my life when I thought I had all the answers, only to discover much later that I had completely missed the wisdom God was trying to offer me.

One of the most significant moments in my life where I truly began to embrace godly wisdom came after a particularly difficult season in business. I had been running on my own understanding, making decisions based on what I believed was best, trusting solely in my experience and instincts. But when things began to unravel—unexpectedly, yet not entirely out of the blue—I was forced to confront the reality that I had been leaning heavily on my own wisdom, not on God's. It was a humbling, even painful realization. But more than that, it was a turning point in my journey.

In that moment of humbling, I began to embrace the wisdom that comes from God alone. I started seeking Him more intentionally, consulting His Word before making decisions, and inviting His Spirit to guide me. That difficult season, as challenging as it was, became the catalyst for a deeper understanding of what it truly means to walk in godly wisdom. It wasn't just about avoiding mistakes—it was about living with a heart that is fully surrendered to God's leading, even when it doesn't align with what I think is best.

Role Models in Scripture

Solomon is perhaps the most well-known example of someone who embraced godly wisdom, and his story offers a powerful lesson for all of us. When Solomon became king of Israel, he was given the opportunity to ask God for anything—wealth, power, influence. But instead of asking for worldly success, Solomon asked for wisdom. In 1 Kings 3:9, Solomon prays, *"So give Your servant a discerning heart to govern Your people and to distinguish between right and wrong."* Solomon understood that the responsibility of leading God's people required more than just strategy or human intellect—it required divine wisdom.

God was so pleased with Solomon's request that He not only granted him unparalleled wisdom, but also wealth and honor beyond what Solomon had asked for. Solomon's reign was marked by peace and prosperity, and his wisdom became legendary, drawing rulers and seekers from around the world to hear his insights.

Solomon's story teaches us that embracing godly wisdom means prioritizing it above all else. It requires us to humble ourselves, recognizing that we don't have all the answers, and to seek God's guidance in every aspect of our lives. When we, like Solomon, put wisdom at the forefront—over wealth, overpower, over personal gain—we open ourselves to God's deeper purpose and plan for our lives. Embracing godly wisdom means allowing God to lead, even when His ways challenge our understanding. It's about recognizing that true wisdom flows not from us, but from the One who holds all understanding and truth.

Scriptures to Remember

"If any of you lacks wisdom, you should ask God, who gives generously to all without finding fault, and it will be given to you."
—James 1:5

"For the Lord gives wisdom; from His mouth come knowledge and understanding."
—Proverbs 2:6

"Wisdom is a shelter as money is a shelter, but the advantage of knowledge is this: Wisdom preserves those who have it."
—Ecclesiastes 7:12

Consider This

Are you embracing godly wisdom in your life, or are you relying on your own understanding? Reflect on Solomon's request for wisdom and how God honored his humility. How can you begin to prioritize godly wisdom in your decisions?

Questions for Reflection

1. How have you been relying on your own wisdom rather than seeking God's guidance?

_____

_____

_____

2. What steps can you take to embrace godly wisdom more fully in your life?

_____

_____

_____

3. How does Solomon's story encourage you to seek God's wisdom in your decisions?

_____

_____

_____

Living Into Our Identity

As children of God, we are called to seek His wisdom in all things. Embracing godly wisdom means humbling ourselves and acknowledging that God's ways are higher than ours. Like Solomon, we can ask God for wisdom, trusting that He will guide us in every decision.

_____

_____

_____

_____

Building Deeper Connection to Faith

- Journaling Prompt: Reflect on an area of your life where you have been relying on your own wisdom. How can you begin to seek God's wisdom in that area instead?
- Prayer: "Lord, give me the humility to embrace Your wisdom in every area of my life. Help me to seek Your guidance and trust in Your understanding, rather than my own. Teach me to rely on You fully as I make decisions, and give me the discernment to know what is right. Amen."

Embracing godly wisdom is a lifelong journey of humility and trust. Like Solomon, we must continually ask God for the wisdom we lack, knowing He gives generously to those who seek Him. Wisdom allows us to navigate life's complexities with discernment, aligning our hearts with God's will. As we grow in wisdom, we make decisions that honor Him and bring peace to our lives. Remember, wisdom is not a one-time request but a daily pursuit that shapes every part of our journey with God.

Tomorrow's Journey

Tomorrow, we'll wrap up our exploration by reflecting on how embracing wisdom prepares us for long-term growth in faith. We'll discuss practical ways to live out the lessons learned and apply wisdom in everyday decisions.

WEEK 3 REFLECTION

As we come to the end of Week 3, take some time to reflect on the lessons you've learned about wisdom and faith. How has this week's study impacted your trust in God's plan? Have you found areas in your life where you need to embrace godly wisdom more fully? Use the following reflection questions to guide your thoughts and journaling.

Reflection Questions

1. How has your understanding of wisdom and faith deepened this week?

    _____

    _____

    _____

2. What steps have you taken to trust God's plan in your decisions?

    _____

    _____

    _____

3. In what areas of your life are you still struggling to embrace godly wisdom?

    _____

    _____

    _____

4. How has faith helped you overcome fear in your decisions?

_____

_____

_____

5. How can you continue to seek God's wisdom in your daily life?

_____

_____

_____

Personal Reflections

1. What specific steps can I take to continue applying wisdom and faith to my decisions?

_____

_____

_____

2. How can I incorporate the lessons from this week into my daily walk with God?

_____

_____

_____

3. Are there any areas where I still struggle to trust God's plan? How can I address those areas?

_____

_____

_____

Action Plan

List three practical actions you will take in the coming week to continue growing in wisdom and faith:

1. _____

   _____

2. _____

   _____

3. _____

   _____

PRAYER

"Lord, thank You for the wisdom You have given me this week. Help me to continue trusting Your plan and walking in faith, even when I don't understand the way ahead. Give me the courage to choose faith over fear, and the humility to seek Your wisdom in every decision. Amen."

This brings your study to a close, but the journey doesn't end here. May the wisdom and faith you've cultivated through this time together continue to guide and shape you in every decision you make. As you move forward, carry these truths with you, allowing them to anchor your steps and deepen your trust in God. Remember, wisdom is not a destination but a lifelong pursuit—one that will guide you closer to God's heart with each passing day. Let this be the beginning of a deeper walk in faith and a continuous seeking of godly wisdom in all areas of your life!

PREPARING FOR THE FUTURE

As we close this study, it's important to recognize that the journey doesn't end here. Wisdom is not a one-time achievement but a lifelong pursuit. The lessons you've learned through this study are meant to be stepping-stones for continued growth. Each decision you make in the future will offer an opportunity to apply the godly wisdom you've gained, drawing you closer to God's plan for your life.

In the weeks and months to come, you will undoubtedly face new challenges, unexpected situations, and decisions that require discernment. It's easy to fall back into old patterns of relying on our understanding or following the world's way of doing things. But now you are equipped with a new perspective—a wisdom that is grounded in faith, prayer, and trust in God's unfailing Word.

Remember that wisdom doesn't mean knowing everything. It means seeking God's guidance, even when you're unsure or afraid. It's about stepping forward in faith, confident that He will lead you through every situation. As you prepare for the future, commit to a life of continued learning, trusting, and growing in your relationship with God.

Key Steps for Moving Forward

1. Keep God at the Center: Make it a daily practice to seek God first in every decision, no matter how big or small. Trust that His wisdom will always guide you to the right path.
2. Be Willing to Wait: Remember that patience and waiting are part of walking in wisdom. Don't rush decisions, but allow God's perfect timing to unfold in your life.
3. Stay Rooted in Scripture: Continue to immerse yourself in God's Word, allowing His truth to shape your thoughts, actions, and decisions. Wisdom comes from knowing and applying the Word.
4. Surround Yourself with Wise Counsel: As you move forward, make sure to seek out mentors, friends, and family members who share your commitment to godly wisdom. They will encourage and guide you in times of need.

The road ahead is full of possibilities, and by living a life centered on wisdom, you will experience the fullness of God's blessings and the peace that comes from knowing He is in control. Keep pressing forward, trusting in the One who holds your future in His hands.

Embracing Wisdom Daily

Wisdom is not something we attain once and then possess forever—it's a daily journey, a continual practice of aligning our thoughts, actions, and decisions with God's guidance. Wisdom requires humility to recognize that we don't have all the answers, and it calls for the discernment to seek God's will in all aspects of our lives. In a world filled with distractions, noise, and quick fixes, embracing wisdom daily becomes a choice to prioritize God's eternal truths over fleeting worldly knowledge.

Living in wisdom is more than just knowing the right thing to do—it's having the courage to do it. It's choosing to walk in God's ways when the world pulls us in the opposite direction. It's being mindful of our words, careful in our actions, and thoughtful in our decisions. Wisdom allows us to navigate the complexities of life with grace, confidence, and peace, knowing that God's hand is guiding us.

Each day offers countless opportunities to either react based on impulse or to pause, reflect, and act with wisdom. The more we embrace this godly wisdom, the more we will see it transform not just our decisions, but our relationships, our faith, and the overall direction of our lives. Wisdom is not just for the big, life-altering decisions—it's also for the everyday moments that shape who we are becoming in Christ.

Key Practices for Embracing Wisdom

- **Daily Prayer for Guidance:** Start each morning by seeking God's wisdom for the day ahead. Ask Him to open your heart and mind to His guidance in both the small and significant decisions you'll face. *"If any of you lacks wisdom, you should ask God, who gives generously to all without finding fault, and it will be given to you"* (James 1:5).
- **Reflection on Scripture:** Commit to spending time in the Word, specifically meditating on passages that speak to wisdom, like Proverbs, Ecclesiastes, and James. These books provide rich insights into how to live wisely and align our choices with God's heart. Reflecting on these truths daily will sharpen your spiritual discernment.
- **Seek Wise Counsel:** Surround yourself with godly friends, mentors, and spiritual leaders who can offer wise counsel. Just

as iron sharpens iron, the wisdom of others can refine your perspective and encourage you to make decisions that are aligned with God's will. Don't be afraid to ask for advice when you need it.

- **Practice Patience and Stillness**: Wisdom often requires waiting on God's timing. In moments of uncertainty, resist the urge to rush or force a decision. Instead, lean into patience, trusting that God's timing is perfect. "*Be still before the Lord and wait patiently for him*" (Psalm 37:7).

- **Mind Your Words:** Proverbs teaches us that "*the tongue has the power of life and death" (Proverbs 18:21)*. Embracing wisdom means being mindful of what we say and how we say it. Use your words to build up, encourage, and speak truth—reflecting God's wisdom in your conversations.

- **Evaluate Your Decisions:** Take time at the end of each day to reflect on your decisions. Were they rooted in wisdom or influenced by external pressures? This practice of evaluation will help you grow in your discernment and refine your ability to make godly choices in the future.

The Impact of Embracing Wisdom Daily

When we commit to seeking wisdom daily, it begins to transform our entire outlook on life. We start to see beyond immediate gratification and short-term gains, focusing instead on long-term impact and eternal significance. Wisdom teaches us to act with integrity, to love without conditions, and to live with purpose.

It also strengthens our faith. Each decision we make, grounded in wisdom, builds our trust in God. It shows us that His ways are always higher than ours and that by leaning on His understanding rather than our own, we are guided on a path that leads to peace and fulfillment. As we embrace wisdom, we begin to notice the fruits of our decisions—stronger relationships, clearer direction, and a deeper connection with God.

By incorporating these daily practices, wisdom will not only shape your actions but also refine your heart. The more we seek God's wisdom, the more we become a reflection of His love and truth in the world around us. Wisdom is a gift that grows with every step we take toward God's perfect will. It transforms how we approach challenges, how we engage with others, and how we live out our calling as followers of Christ.

When we embrace wisdom daily, we live with purpose, confidence, and the assurance that God is guiding every step.

Continuing the Journey

As you come to the close of this study on wisdom, it's essential to recognize that the journey of wisdom doesn't end here. Wisdom is not a destination you arrive at—it is an ongoing process of growth, learning, and transformation. Each day presents new opportunities to apply the principles of wisdom you've learned, and each moment offers the chance to seek God's guidance and align your decisions with His will.

The truth is, life will always present us with challenges and choices, some that feel overwhelming and others that seem routine. But in every decision, no matter how big or small, wisdom invites us to slow down, reflect, and seek God's direction. This journey of wisdom is about cultivating a heart that is sensitive to God's voice, a mind that discerns His truth, and a spirit that is willing to follow His lead.

What You've Gained

Through this study, you've gained more than just knowledge—you've gained the tools to navigate life's complexities with the wisdom of God. You've learned to distinguish between worldly knowledge and godly wisdom, to seek counsel, to embrace humility, to speak wisely, and to wait patiently on God's timing. These lessons will serve as a foundation for your continued growth in Christ.

But this is just the beginning. Wisdom, like faith, is something we must nurture. It's a practice that requires consistency, humility, and a constant reliance on God's Word. There will be moments when you stumble, when decisions don't go as planned, or when you find yourself relying more on your understanding than God's wisdom. In those moments, remember that wisdom is not about perfection—it's about progression. It's about choosing, each day, to seek God's truth and to live by His principles.

Continuing to Grow in Wisdom

As you continue your journey, here are a few practical steps to help you grow in wisdom:

- **Commit to Ongoing Study of God's Word**: The Bible is the ultimate source of wisdom, offering insights and guidance for every aspect of life. Make it a daily habit to dive into Scripture, especially the books of Proverbs, Ecclesiastes, and James. These texts are rich with lessons on living wisely and will help keep your heart aligned with God's wisdom.
- **Surround Yourself with Wise Counsel:** Wisdom is often cultivated in community. Stay connected with fellow believers who challenge and encourage you in your walk with Christ.

Seek out mentors who can offer guidance and perspective, and be willing to listen when they share their wisdom with you.

- **Stay Rooted in Prayer:** Wisdom begins with seeking God in prayer. Make prayer a daily priority, asking God to give you discernment, to lead you in your decisions, and to help you apply the lessons you've learned. Trust that He will guide you as you continue to seek His heart.
- **Embrace Humility:** Remember that wisdom is grounded in humility. It's the recognition that we don't have all the answers, but that God does. Approach each decision with a posture of humility, willing to learn and grow from whatever God has to teach you in that moment.
- **Apply Wisdom Daily:** Wisdom is not just for the major crossroads of life—it's for the everyday moments. Practice wisdom in how you speak, how you interact with others, and how you manage your time, resources, and relationships. The more you apply wisdom in the small things, the more prepared you will be to make wise choices in the bigger things.

A Life Shaped by Wisdom

As you move forward, let wisdom shape the way you live. Let it guide your decisions, strengthen your relationships, and deepen your faith. The wisdom you seek from God is not just for your benefit—it's for the benefit of those around you. As you grow in wisdom, you become a light to others, helping them see the goodness and faithfulness of God.

God promises to give wisdom generously to those who ask for it. So, keep asking. Keep seeking. Keep growing. Let wisdom be the foundation on which you build your life, trusting that God will continue to guide your steps as you pursue Him.

Remember, wisdom is not a one-time achievement—it's a lifelong pursuit. As you continue to walk this journey, know that God is with you every step of the way, offering His guidance, His peace, and His wisdom in abundance.

May the wisdom you've gained continue to bless and guide you as you journey forward, and may it overflow into every area of your life, leading you closer to God and to His perfect will.

Embrace the Lifelong Journey

As we conclude this study, it's important to acknowledge that the pursuit of wisdom doesn't have an endpoint—it's a lifelong journey. In every season of life, wisdom invites us to grow, to learn, and to deepen our trust in God's plan. Just as we grow physically, emotionally, and spiritually, we are also called to grow in wisdom, maturing in how we approach life's challenges and decisions.

The wisdom you've gained throughout this study is not meant to be stored away or used only in critical moments. It's something to live out every day. Wisdom is woven into the fabric of daily life—how we treat others, how we speak, how we manage our time, and how we respond to both joy and adversity. Embracing wisdom is a decision to live with intentionality, reflecting God's heart in every choice we make.

Wisdom for Every Season

Life is a series of seasons—some full of joy, others marked by difficulty. No matter what season you find yourself in, wisdom is your constant companion, helping you navigate with grace and discernment. In times of celebration, wisdom reminds us to remain humble and grateful. In seasons of struggle, wisdom points us back to God's promises, guiding us to make decisions grounded in faith rather than fear.

As you move forward, remember that wisdom is not something that develops all at once. It's built over time, through daily surrender to God's guidance and a heart that seeks His will above all else. The Bible tells us in Proverbs 4:7, "The beginning of wisdom is this: Get wisdom. Though it cost all you have, get understanding." This is the call of wisdom—to seek it, to treasure it, and to never stop pursuing it.

A Heart That Seeks Wisdom

Living a life marked by wisdom requires a heart that is willing to seek it continually. This means creating space in your daily life to connect with God, to meditate on His Word, and to reflect on His truths. It means surrounding yourself with wise counsel and remaining open to correction and growth. It also means cultivating a spirit of humility, recognizing that wisdom is a gift from God and not something we achieve on our own.

When we embrace the lifelong journey of wisdom, we allow God to shape us into the people He has called us to be. It's not about perfection, but about progress—learning, growing, and becoming more like Christ with each step we take.

How to Continue Your Journey

1. **Daily Surrender:** Each day, commit to seeking God's wisdom in all areas of your life. Whether through prayer, Bible study, or quiet reflection, invite God to guide your thoughts, words, and actions.

2. **Seek Wise Counsel:** Continue to surround yourself with mentors, friends, and spiritual leaders who can offer godly advice and guidance. Don't be afraid to ask for help when faced with difficult decisions.

3. **Remain Teachable:** Wisdom requires a humble and teachable spirit. Be open to learning, to correction, and to growth. Embrace the process, knowing that God is continually refining you.

4. **Reflect on Your Journey:** Take time regularly to reflect on the lessons you've learned, the growth you've experienced, and the ways God has worked through your pursuit of wisdom. Journaling is a great way to document your journey and to see how God is shaping your life over time.

5. **Pass It On:** Wisdom is not just for your benefit. As you grow in wisdom, look for opportunities to share what you've learned with others. Be a source of encouragement, guidance, and support for those around you.

The Impact of a Wise Life

A life lived in wisdom is a life that reflects God's goodness to the world. Your choices, your words, and your actions all have the potential to influence those around you for the better. As you continue to grow in wisdom, you'll find that your life becomes a testimony to God's faithfulness. You will inspire others to seek wisdom, to live with purpose, and to trust in God's plan for their lives.

As you move forward, remember that the journey of wisdom is never over. Each new day brings new opportunities to seek God's wisdom and to live it out. So, continue to embrace this journey with faith and confidence, trusting that God will guide your steps and lead you into the fullness of His plans.

May your life be a reflection of His wisdom, and may you continue to grow in grace and knowledge as you walk this lifelong journey.

PRAYER FOR WISDOM:
Making Godly Decisions

Opening:

"Heavenly Father, I come before You with a humble heart, acknowledging Your greatness and the boundless wisdom You offer to guide me through life's decisions."

Thanksgiving:

"Thank You, Lord, for walking with me through this journey of understanding and embracing Your wisdom. I am grateful for the insight, clarity, and discernment You have provided, and for the way Your Word has illuminated my path."

Reflection:

"Lord, I have learned that true wisdom is rooted in You. It's not just knowledge, but understanding and applying Your principles in my everyday life. I now see that godly wisdom requires trust, patience, and the humility to follow Your guidance rather than my own understanding."

Petitions:

> "Father, I ask for Your continued strength and guidance as I strive to make decisions that reflect Your will. Help me to trust Your timing, especially when it's difficult to wait, and to seek Your wisdom in every situation. Fill me with Your Spirit, so that I may approach each choice with discernment, grace, and faith."

Commitment:

> "I commit to seeking Your wisdom in all things, remaining faithful to Your Word and allowing Your truth to direct my steps. Help me to approach each decision with humility, trusting that You will guide me in the way I should go."

Intercession:

> "I also lift up those who are struggling to make decisions in their own lives. May they turn to You for guidance and wisdom. Use me, Lord, as a source of encouragement and support, sharing the wisdom You have given me to help others find peace and clarity."

Closing:

> "I ask all these things in the name of Jesus Christ, my Savior and the source of all wisdom. Amen."

ADDITIONAL RESOURCES FOR WISDOM:
Making Godly Decisions

Books: Suggested Readings for Deeper Understanding

"The Wisdom Pyramid: Feeding Your Soul in a Post-Truth World" by Brett McCracken

This book explores the importance of seeking wisdom in a world overwhelmed by information. McCracken uses the metaphor of a pyramid to help readers structure their intake of knowledge and wisdom, offering practical steps to cultivate a more balanced, wise life.

"The Art of Decision Making: How We Move from Indecision to Smart Choices" by Joseph Bikart

Bikart dives into the psychology and philosophy behind decision-making. This book offers insight into how to develop critical thinking and discernment in complex situations, grounded in wisdom and self-awareness.

"The Way of Wisdom" by Timothy Keller

In this devotional guide, Timothy Keller explores the book of Proverbs and offers reflections on how to apply biblical wisdom in every aspect of daily life. Keller's clear and practical insights help readers build a foundation of wisdom through Scripture.

"God's Wisdom for Navigating Life" by Tim and Kathy Keller
A year-long devotional that unpacks the wisdom of Proverbs, guiding readers to apply its lessons to daily decisions and challenges. This resource encourages readers to rely on God's wisdom in all areas of life.

Articles: Recommended Articles for Further Insight

"Biblical Wisdom for Everyday Decisions" on Christianity Today
This article delves into how Christians can seek wisdom in their decision-making processes, exploring what the Bible says about balancing faith, discernment, and wisdom in daily life.

"Why We Need Godly Wisdom in a Culture of Instant Gratification" on The Gospel Coalition
This article discusses the contrast between biblical wisdom and the fast-paced, instant-result mentality of modern society. It provides actionable advice on how to apply patience and wisdom in today's world.

"Making Wise Decisions in Uncertain Times" on Focus on the Family
Offering insights for navigating difficult decisions, this article reflects on how to seek God's wisdom during times of uncertainty and challenges, highlighting how faith can guide us through indecision.

"The Power of Wisdom in Relationships" on Bible.org

This article explores how godly wisdom shapes the way we interact with others, offering practical tips on applying wisdom to build stronger, more loving relationships.

Online Resources

Christianity Today (www.christianitytoday.com)

A leading resource for Christian news, articles, and spiritual insights, Christianity Today offers a wealth of material focused on how to live wisely in a complex world.

The Gospel Coalition (www.thegospelcoalition.org)

This site features articles, sermons, and resources that emphasize the importance of biblical wisdom in all aspects of life, helping readers navigate modern challenges with a godly perspective.

Focus on the Family (www.focusonthefamily.com)

A well-known Christian resource that provides practical advice on family, relationships, and faith. Focus on the Family offers articles, videos, and resources that can help guide wise decision-making.

Bible.org (www.bible.org)

With study tools, resources, and articles dedicated to exploring the Bible, this site helps readers dive deeper into the Scriptures, including a focus on wisdom, decision-making, and understanding God's guidance.

ABOUT THE AUTHOR

Eric G. Reid, Editor-in-Chief and Co-Founder of Skinny Brown Dog Media, wakes up every day with a passion for guiding others in discovering their identity and purpose. With over a decade of experience in publishing, Eric has helped authors, speakers, and leaders bring their unique voices to life.

As a writer, Eric understands the power of storytelling and the importance of finding your true voice. His journey has been shaped by personal and professional growth, and he is dedicated to walking alongside others on their paths of faith and self-discovery.

When not working, Eric enjoys family time and the companionship of his big yellow dog, Max. He values moments of rest and reflection, which fuel his mission of helping others embrace their God-given identity. You can connect with Eric at Eric@SkinnyBrownDogMedia.com.

ABOUT THE WHOLE LIFE DEVOTIONAL SERIES

Welcome to the Whole Life Devotional Series—your spiritual road trip through different aspects of your faith journey. Each book serves as a personal guide, offering practical insights and biblical wisdom to help you grow in your relationship with God and live a life that truly reflects His love and purpose.

This series isn't about complex theology; it's written in an approachable, relatable way that feels like a conversation with a friend who is passionate about personal growth and faith. Through real-life stories, down-to-earth advice, and scripture, each book aims to help you connect more deeply with God and understand who He has called you to be.

Feel free to reach out to me at Eric@SkinnyBrownDogMedia. com. I would love to hear how these books are helping you along your journey as we grow together in faith.

Books in the Series

Identity: Discovering Who You Are

- Focus: Understanding and embracing your identity in Christ.
- Themes: Self-worth, God's love, being made in God's image.

- Summary: Learn to see yourself through God's eyes and replace the world's misconceptions with the truth of who you are in Christ.

Faith: Strengthening Your Relationship with God

- Focus: Deepening your faith and spiritual growth.
- Themes: Prayer, Bible study, spiritual disciplines.
- Summary: Build a strong, everyday faith that transforms your life and draws you closer to God.

Transformation: Embracing Spiritual Growth

- Focus: Becoming more Christlike through spiritual growth.
- Themes: Spiritual maturity, growth in virtues, sanctification.
- Summary: Experience the ongoing process of spiritual transformation and grow deeper in your walk with God.

Wisdom: Making Godly Decisions

- Focus: Making wise, biblically-based decisions.
- Themes: Discernment, moral choices, God's guidance.
- Summary: Gain the wisdom to make decisions that align with God's will and reflect His wisdom in your daily life.

Surrender: Embracing God's Will

- Focus: Surrendering to God's will.
- Themes: Trust, obedience, letting go, faith.

- Summary: Learn to let go of control and trust in God's perfect plan, embracing His will for your life.

Peace: Finding Rest in a Busy World

- Focus: Finding true rest and peace in God.
- Themes: Stress management, spiritual rest, trust in God.
- Summary: Discover how to find peace and rest through faith, even amidst the busyness of life, and learn to trust in God's provision.

I AM

A SEEKER OF GOD'S WISDOM:
"For the Lord gives wisdom;
from his mouth come knowledge and understanding."
—Proverbs 2:6

ANCHORED IN GOD'S GUIDANCE:
"Trust in the Lord with all your heart and lean not on your own
understanding; in all your ways submit to him,
and he will make your paths straight."
—Proverbs 3:5-6

MADE FOR DISCERNMENT:
"Do not conform to the pattern of this world, but be transformed by the
renewing of your mind. Then you will be able to test and approve what
God's will is—his good, pleasing, and perfect will."
—Romans 12:2

GUIDED BY GODLY COUNSEL:
"Plans fail for lack of counsel, but with many advisers they succeed."
—Proverbs 15:22

WALKING IN GOD'S WAYS:
"Blessed are those who find wisdom, those who gain understanding,
for she is more profitable than silver and yields better returns than gold."
—Proverbs 3:13-14

A LIGHT TO OTHERS THROUGH WISDOM:
"In the same way, let your light shine before others,
that they may see your good deeds and glorify your Father in heaven."
—Matthew 5:16

LIVING WITH THE MIND OF CHRIST:
"For who has known the mind of the Lord so as to instruct him?
But we have the mind of Christ."
—1 Corinthians 2:16

EMBRACING HUMILITY IN WISDOM:
"When pride comes, then comes disgrace,
but with humility comes wisdom."
—Proverbs 11:2

FILLED WITH SPIRITUAL INSIGHT:
"I keep asking that the God of our Lord Jesus Christ,
the glorious Father, may give you the Spirit of wisdom and revelation,
so that you may know him better."
—Ephesians 1:17

TRUSTING IN GOD'S PLAN AND TIMING:
"There is a time for everything,
and a season for every activity under the heavens."
—Ecclesiastes 3:1

GROUNDED IN GOD'S ETERNAL WISDOM:
"Oh, the depth of the riches of the wisdom and knowledge of God!
How unsearchable his judgments, and his paths beyond tracing out!"
—Romans 11:33

GROWING IN WISDOM THROUGH TRIALS:
"If any of you lacks wisdom, you should ask God,
who gives generously to all without finding fault,
and it will be given to you."
—James 1:5

A WITNESS OF GOD'S GOODNESS THROUGH WISE CHOICES:
"Let your light shine before others,
that they may see your good deeds and glorify your Father in heaven."
—Matthew 5:16

STRENGTHENED BY GOD'S WISDOM AND UNDERSTANDING:
"He gives wisdom to the wise and knowledge to the discerning."
—Daniel 2:21

ENTRUSTING MY LIFE TO GOD'S PERFECT WILL:
"'For I know the plans I have for you,' declares the Lord,
'plans to prosper you and not to harm you,
plans to give you hope and a future.'"
—Jeremiah 29:11